Advance T
Gend

Gender Matters is a must read book fc _____ _hilanthropic sector. Intentionally thought-pr _____ ...₌d ıor easy application, Kathleen provides practical tools, relevant frameworks and dynamic stories about how and why we must pay careful attention to women in our overall engagement strategy. Our sector is transforming! Women are giving with the intention of making a real difference locally and globally. This books makes it clear that the time is now for cultivating new relationships with women.

> —**Vanessa Cooksey,** Senior Vice President, Community Relations at Wells
> Fargo and Women's Philanthropy Institute Advisory Board Member

In this engaging discourse on an important topic, Kathleen Loehr identifies the barriers that continue to exist in meeting women philanthropists on their terms, explains why these barriers have persisted, and—most importantly—supplies sound solutions for overcoming a history of misguided approaches. This is an important read for every development professional looking to expand the diversity of their support base and inspire new supporters to their mission.

> —**Jon Thorsen,** Associate Vice President, Advancement Services,
> George Washington University

Do you care about unlocking abundant resources to serve your organization's mission and purpose? Read this book. Finally we have a comprehensive resource to help us understand the power and potential of women's giving. Many of the insights in *Gender Matters* are so present and true for the Women Moving Millions community.

> —**Jacki Zehner,** CoFounder, Women Moving Millions and Former Partner and
> Managing Director, Goldman Sachs

"They" have been writing large checks for years. The actuarial statistics have told us that *women* out live men and often give longer and more over time.

The time for authentic data and direction on this topic is now; the book is here; it is called *Gender Matters,* and *the* person to tell this story is Kathleen Loehr. This treatment of this subject will guide professional and volunteer thinking on women in philanthropy for the coming decades and reflects Kathleen's rich experiences in this arena. Read it for sure, but most vitally, put its wisdom into your planning. The results will speak for themselves because gender really does matter!

> —**Bob Carter,** Past Chair, AFP International Board; Past CEO, Ketchum, Inc.;
> Chair & Founder, Carter.Global

Kathleen Loehr has taken her 25 years of experience in women's giving and has turned it into a book full of research data, successful examples and most importantly—tangible advice on how to design a program unique to your challenges. Organizations make many mistakes as they begin to focus on cultivating women donors, Kathleen identifies them and shares strategies to avoid them. She also shares the most successful methods for increasing giving from women donors. Whether you have been fundraising for decades like me, or just getting started—take time to read this book, your bottom line will be grateful that you did.

—**Linda Paulson,** Vice President, Philanthropic Engagement, Washington Area Women's Foundation

As Kathleen points out, knowledge alone does not cause change and so she presents practical advice, relatable stories and a clear path forward for engaging women donors in ways that can truly impact your organization and in turn, our civil society. Her years in the field provides a deep well of "real world" experience which she expertly balances with solid data to provide the perfect blend of heart and head. A valuable read for those who recognize the possibilities of engaging women donors with an approach that can also be applied to other donor populations.

—**Henry L. Berman,** Ed.D, CEO, Exponent Philanthropy

Kathleen Loehr challenges us all to dig deep and look hard at what is getting in the way of growing women's philanthropy. *Gender Matters* is a timely book that does not pretend that cookie-cutter solutions will work. It provides a sustainable approach to help design what will work for *your* organization to increase significant gifts and support.

—**Jennifer Dumas,** Director of Principal Gifts

Kathleen Loehr's work is genius—it raises the curtain on how women are absolutely central to successful fundraising endeavors at universities and organizations around the globe. Katherine provides practical advice for fundraisers as they create a robust roadmap for their women and philanthropy efforts. This is a must-read book.

—**Sue Gerdelman,** Campaign Chair, For the Bold Campaign, The College of William & Mary

Kathleen Loehr so cogently puts in words what we as women philanthropic leaders intuitively know—gender absolutely matters in philanthropic decision-making. Loehr's inquiry-based analysis of how fundraisers can collaboratively discover, dream, design, and create destiny for women philanthropists is a game-changer in how we think of approaches to gender-based giving.

—**Judy Altenberg,** Immediate Past Chair, National Women's Philanthropy, Jewish Federations of North America

At the National Coalition of Girls' Schools, we know beyond a doubt that gender matters in school, work and life. I also know that it matters in philanthropy—women do give differently. I am grateful that Kathleen Loehr provides a clear and compelling guide to help us all grow the varied resources women can provide to create lasting change. The leaders of girls' schools have been asking for a specific manual on how to adjust our fundraising practices for women—we now have it thanks to this book.

—**Megan Murphy,** Executive Director, National Coalition of Girls' Schools

Kathleen Loehr has written an important and timely book that will help all of us deepen our understanding of women's philanthropy and organizational change. Institutions with intentions to expand their focus on women donors have a road-map; institutions with established programs have an invaluable guide for creating sustainable organizational change. Loehr goes beyond her insightful and intelligent discussion of approaches, tools, and concepts to why and how we can transform our advancement enterprises for a future where women are in the forefront of giving. A must read for everyone thinking about the nature of philanthropy in the 21st century!

—**Laurie Burns McRobbie,** First Lady, Indiana University,
   Founder, IU Women's Philanthropy

Kathleen Loehr has written a magnificent opus on women's philanthropy. She brings the latest research to the topic and breaks the myths that have long haunted the subject of women's charitable behavior. It is not just a "how to" book on raising funds from a critically important demographic, but a book that expands the reader's understanding of what is possible if we dream big.

—**Ellen Remmer,** Senior Partner at The Philanthropic Initiative,
   President of the Remmer Family Foundation

There is no better time for Kathleen Loehr's important new book on women and philan-thropy. Loehr skillfully relates how traditional fundraising practices evolved, why they no longer fit, and how nonprofits leave money on the table when they ignore gender differences. Packed with insight and brimming with actionable ideas, *Gender Matters* should be required reading for nonprofit staff, board, and fundraisers in any sector.

—**Cindy Cox Roman,** HelpAge USA board member, HelpAge Global
   Ambassador, and CEO, WIT Consulting LLC

Kathleen Loehr has been a strong proponent of women's philanthropy for many years. Through *Gender Matters* she adds the moniker of women's philanthropy curator to her resume. The definition of curator is one who selects, organizes and looks after the items in a collection or exhibition. Loehr takes much of the data and research stemming from places like the Women's Philanthropy Institute at the Lilly

Family School of Philanthropy, and looks after it with a keen eye and articulation for both theory and practice. The book is designed to be a collection of better principles (as opposed to best practices) that fundraisers should consider as they seek to expand their donor base by paying closer attention to the ways women and other under-represented constituents make charitable decisions and take subsequent action. Loehr's conversational style makes it an easy read; her practical advice makes it an essential guidebook for the future of philanthropy!

—**Patricia P. Jackson,** Interim Vice President for Development & Alumni Relations at Geisel School of Medicine and Dartmouth-Hitchcock Health

Women have been donors since time immemorial, but their generosity, and ways of practicing giving, has been largely unrecognized and lauded. Beginning in the early nineties, efforts by the Women's Philanthropy Institute began calling attention to the significant value of women's giving, and at the same time, pointing out differences in gender giving which can be backed up by research and experience. As someone who is devoted to donor diversity, I am highly pleased that we have an up-to-date volume that will guide us in taking women's giving to yet another, high level, with the accompanying recognition it deserves, and therefore can also highly recommend this book.

—**Dr. Lilya Wagner,** Director of Philanthropic Service for Institutions for the Seventh-day Adventist Church North America Division

As the Executive Director of a woman's organization whose goal is to raise money from women to support women the information and insight contained in this book is invaluable. This impactful book not only provides the tools and resources for us to Dream, Design, and Deliver but Kathleen engages her readers to want to learn how we can become better fundraisers. Thank you Kathleen for bringing to the forefront such an important issue that is crucial to the success of women's philanthropy. I am confident that our Foundation will have greater success in our fundraising efforts because of Kathleen and this book.

—**Amy Peebles,** Executive Director, Alpha Phi Foundation

Kathleen provides incredibly unique insights to women in philanthropy. I have learned from her that women view philanthropy in a manner that bucks the traditional male driven approaches, including means of engagement, stewardship and donor solicitation. We have partnered on many assignments that have capitalized on this skill-set and as a result, I have adapted my approach and have become more sensitive to the interests of women who want to have a greater impact.

—**Stephen K. Orr,** Managing Partner and Co-Founder, Orr Associates, Inc. (OAI)

Gender Matters

A GUIDE TO

Growing Women's Philanthropy

Kathleen E. Loehr

COUNCIL FOR ADVANCEMENT
AND SUPPORT OF EDUCATION®

London • Mexico City • Singapore • Washington, DC

© 2018 Council for Advancement and Support of Education
ISBN10: 089964-552-6
ISBN13: 978-0-89964-552-6

Printed in the United States of America

COUNCIL FOR ADVANCEMENT
AND SUPPORT OF EDUCATION®

London · Mexico City · Singapore · Washington, DC

Advancing education to transform lives and society.

www.case.org

TABLE OF CONTENTS

FOREWORD

At the Women's Philanthropy Institute, we regularly say that gender matters in philanthropy. Men and women have different motivations for giving and different patterns of giving. One is not better than the other; they are simply different. Not only does Kathleen Loehr embody that message throughout her book, she argues persuasively that it is time to pay more attention to women as philanthropists.

If ever there was a time for THIS book, it is now. American society has changed and continues to change rapidly. The United States is growing more diverse racially and ethnically, a trend that will continue for the next half century, according to the Pew Research Center (http://www.pewresearch .org/fact-tank/2016/03/31/10-demographic-trends-that-are-shaping-the-u-s -and-the-world/). Generational shifts are occurring with the millennials (1981–1996) surpassing baby boomers (1946–1964) in 2016 as the largest living generation. At the same time, women have come into their own in this country—in business and politics, and increasingly in philanthropy. Amidst these sea changes, Kathleen offers a clear, powerful way forward for fundraisers and other nonprofit leaders to welcome more diverse donors, including women, to join in their organization's mission.

The advantages to this way forward are clear. By embracing the changes around us rather than remaining static or in denial of the changes, we will engage more potential donors, generate more buzz around our missions and raise more money to fulfill those missions. It's that simple.

Kathleen has woven the research about gender differences in philanthropy throughout the book, using the data points to inform practice exactly as we had envisioned how the Women's Philanthropy Institute research might be applied. Her many examples bring the research to life, using it as the framework to help fundraisers and other nonprofit leaders imagine what's possible.

Gender Matters does not ask fundraisers to start from scratch. Rather, Loehr asks nonprofits to dream big and to concentrate on how to engage more diverse stakeholders in designing strategies to achieve that dream. The appreciative inquiry model used in the book works because Loehr builds on the awareness and understanding that each nonprofit institution has a culture, goals and objectives unique to it. Instead of offering a prix fixe menu, she presents a la carte choices so that readers can create roadmaps suitable to their organization's unique characteristics and then build and implement strategies slowly or more rapidly but always intentionally.

Kathleen introduced the appreciative inquiry model to the Women's Philanthropy Institute and we have used it to achieve new levels of excellence. You can, too. With some adjustment, the examples she shares can be used by leaders across the nonprofit sector to guide critical thinking and action around many pressing issues.

We are grateful to Kathleen not only for this book, which provides a clear path forward to accelerate women's philanthropy and increase much needed resources for a nonprofit sector that is being called on to do more and more, but also for her years of service (nine and counting) as a founding member of the WPI Council. We can always count on her to ask, "for the sake of what" at meetings and in conversations. Why does it matter? What will be different when we do this?

Why does this book matter? What will be different after reading it?

- Fundraisers will use the demographics about women and research data to spark more conversations about gender differences in charitable giving behavior within and outside the organization, to assess what is possible, and to drive strategic change in their work.
- More and more nonprofits will act on this wake-up call and engage women donors in ways that acknowledge their preferences.
- Strategies for engaging diverse donors—including women—will be fully integrated within and across all fundraising practices from the annual fund to principal gifts and from prospect research and stewardship to marketing and communications.
- Fundraisers and donors alike will ramp up storytelling about women stepping fully into their philanthropy as Kathleen models in her intro-

duction with the powerful stories of Kathryn Vecellio and Agnes Gund. These stories will prompt new philanthropic behavior from other women as they see more role models and, collectively, we will elevate recognition of women as society's change makers.

- As more fundraisers embrace what's possible through the appreciative inquiry model, they will move confidently in alignment with a broader base of donors—men and women of all ages, races, ethnicities, sexual orientation—to raise more funds to meet today's and tomorrow's challenges.

Kathleen has written a book that is clearly for this time, for now. It is not prescriptive. It is forward thinking. It asks the reader to pay attention to the demographics and the research and act on the data in a thoughtful way that is reflective of the institution's history, culture, and values. It asks us to bring our heads, our hearts and our hands to this important work. And, in doing so, we have the potential to change the world.

Debra Mesch, Ph.D.
Director, Women's Philanthropy Institute
Eileen Lamb O'Gara Chair in
Women's Philanthropy

Andrea Pactor
Associate Director
Women's Philanthropy Institute

INTRODUCTION

This book is predicated on a straightforward premise. Our efforts to raise philanthropic funds are missing significant support from half of our population—women. Everyone who cares about philanthropy should care about women and how they give. The time has come to elevate and accelerate women's philanthropy.

To help make this case, I will start with two representative stories.

The Cleveland Clinic Florida understands that paying attention to the other half of the population can mean the difference between life and death. The hospital is one of the few institutions in the United States that provides comprehensive cardiovascular medical care to women. It also has the largest database tracking gender difference in valve disease. In early 2018, the hospital announced a $1 million gift to increase research in women's cardiology. Businesswoman Kathryn Vecellio made the gift with her husband to establish the Kathryn C. and Leo A. Vecellio Cardiology Research Fund. Due to personal experience, Kathryn is a passionate advocate for women's heart health. She said she and her husband wanted to "provide Cleveland Clinic with the means to support innovative research and recruit and retain more clinicians specializing in women's cardiovascular health." This is the second gift from this family and is in addition to Kathryn's longtime engagement as a volunteer and advocate with Cleveland Clinic Florida (Donnelly 2018).

In another example of women's philanthropic impact, Agnes Gund, the president emerita of the Museum of Modern Art, created the Art for Justice

Fund in 2017. Gund established the fund in partnership with the Ford Foundation with $100 million of the proceeds from the $165 million sale of a Roy Lichtenstein painting. The goal was to support criminal justice reform and reduce mass incarceration in the United States through the sale of valuable art. *The New York Times* reported in 2017:

> "This is one thing I can do before I die," Ms. Gund said in an interview when the fund was created. "This is what I need to do." Ms. Gund challenged fellow collectors to use their artwork to champion social causes. Nearly 30 other donors have made contributions of at least $100,000 to the fund, organizers say, and the plan is for all of the fund's money to be distributed over the next five years.

Within six months of its inception, the fund gave $22 million in grants, ranging in size from $100,000 to $7.5 million, to thirty programs (Libbey 2017).

Here is a woman philanthropist bringing innovation, assets (art), partnership (with the Ford Foundation), collaboration (encouraging others to give as well) and swift decision-making to address the high rates of incarceration and recidivism in the United States. Gund demonstrates that women bring many resources to the table of change; money is just one.

I believe that thousands more of these stories are possible for every university and nonprofit in this country if they equip their fundraising programs to fully integrate women and the distinct ways they give.

I have been a fundraiser for more than 35 years, in the field of women's philanthropy for 22 years and a philanthropic strategist for 10 years. I was trained by Martha Taylor and Sondra Shaw-Hardy in the same year they came out with their seminal book *Reinventing Fundraising: Realizing the Potential of Women's Philanthropy.* As the director of the President's Council of Cornell Women in 1996, I relied on their advice to work with more than 400 powerful, networked and committed alumnae who cared deeply about the university. I continued to use Taylor and Shaw-Hardy's principles to engage women when I was a leader at the American Red Cross and, later, with numerous universities and nonprofits.

The Women's Philanthropy Institute at the Lilly Family School of Philanthropy at Indiana University has been around in various forms for over 25 years. WPI provides deep research on women's giving, which is frequently quoted in national media to show that gender matters. And yet, despite these documented differences, we often still apply the same approach to most donors, regardless of age, gender, sexual orientation or ethnicity.

Thanks to research through the WPI, we now know that women drive philanthropic decisions in many, perhaps most, families. They give more than men do. They give differently. We know that this trend will continue, given the growth of women's earnings and the inheritances they will receive, often twice— once from their parents and again from their spouses or partners.

Taylor and Shaw-Hardy's astuteness and the continued research from WPI have certainly made our country realize the potential of women's philanthropy.

However, we have not yet reinvented fundraising to build meaningful relationships with women. We are not matching our increased understanding of how women give with updated fundraising practices. This book shows us how to fill that gap.

Our sector is behind the times. Consumer companies have adapted their behaviors for women. This shows up in their targeted marketing. Proctor and Gamble, for instance, produced for the 2018 Winter Olympics memorable ads about the mothers of athletes. This was not about doing a "nice" ad. It was designed to connect to their primary consumer base, women. Financial advisors are trained to understand how women make investment decisions differently than men. These are simply examples of good business aimed at increasing the bottom line. The people who work in these professions understand that women control most of the wealth in this country and are their households' chief financial officers.

In contrast, the clear majority of nonprofits and universities still use fundraising practices that either turn off women or gain only minimal support from them. So much more is possible.

As fundraisers, we are well practiced in repeating specific actions to raise money successfully each year. These practices work well. We raise billions and that serves to reinforce our behavior. We don't stop to consider that "best practices" designed for one specific group may not be the best approach for the many other types of donors we'd like to engage. That is what this book is about.

We are what we practice. This means we choose behaviors to achieve a goal we desire, practice them over and over and, at some point, we can effortlessly, almost unconsciously, gain the same result regularly without thinking. Consider, for example, driving a car. We go from interest in driving, to learning how to drive, to practicing over and over, to then driving without thinking. And once we learn to drive, we are drivers. This is the embodiment of skills that serve us.

When there are new opportunities and new results we desire, it's time to learn new skills. This takes awareness and practice. Say you want to learn to ride cross country on a motorcycle. Although it, too, is a vehicle, knowing how to drive a car does not automatically make you a competent motorcyclist. You'll need to acquire new skills—proper body positioning for balance, a heightened awareness of surrounding traffic and greater attentiveness to road and weather conditions that may present safety hazards. You will practice these new skills, first with awkwardness, then with greater ease. In time, you are effortlessly doing something you previously could not. You are a motorcyclist.

We want to transform as fundraisers to connect to the greater diversity of donors in our portfolios. Simply knowing about how donor groups give differently is clearly not enough to change how we relate to them and gain significant and sustained support and funding. Change doesn't happen when we've gained knowledge. Change happens when we use that knowledge to engage in new practices that alter who we are and how we appear to others. Only when we consistently act differently will we begin to optimize how we raise more money from many more types of donors.

We all have a role to play to increase diversity in our sector. Some leaders are tackling the fact that boards are not reflective of today's donors. Others are focused on new hiring techniques to increase diversity in staff. There are many aspects of our profession that need attention and adaptation, so we can align with today's staff, volunteer leaders and donors to build the trusted, supportive relationships that will fuel our missions for decades to come.

The role of this book is to spotlight current fundraising behaviors with women and how we can adapt to increase their support. I write about women's philanthropy not just because it is my area of expertise, but because women are the fastest growing philanthropic group with wealth, commitment to change and influence. Women are where the dollars and decision-making are now and will be for some time. I know that women are just one part of the large, complex world of donors today, but they are half our population. I believe focusing on women is a logical first step for any organization looking to diversify its fundraising practices.

This Book

I purposely stayed away from writing a "how to" book, since linear, simple solutions are not the answer. Humans are not widgets. We cannot design the top ten "If X, then Y" strategies to get the results we desire. I've witnessed the frustration and lost income that results from simply applying tactical processes to cultivate women donors.

I also know that each organization has a rich, unique culture and design. How a fundraising environment grows within each culture is dynamic, which means that tailored, sustainable solutions are needed to grow women's support within an individual organization. I'll share in a later chapter the lost momentum that occurred when a "solution for women stakeholders" was simply added to the traditional culture and beliefs. I'll also write about the benefit of a whole system approach.

If you are one of those people, like me, who thumbs through a book looking for a plan of action, I encourage you to start with the front sections. No simple solutions will work without awareness of the facts about women donors in the United States, deep listening to *your* women stakeholders and choosing the specific goals that are best for your organization.

With all this in mind, I wrote this book within an *Appreciative Inquiry* framework. Appreciative Inquiry was created by David Cooperrider in the 1980s and is a well-researched, effective design model that consistently leads to sustained change in organizations. Appreciative Inquiry theory focuses on organizations as centers of human relatedness. Practitioners have found over and over that when people understand and see the potential in others, and are connected in new ways, unimaginable change can occur. Cooperrider writes:

> In [Appreciative Inquiry], intervention gives way to inquiry, imagination, and innovation. Instead of negation, criticism and spiraling diagnosis, there is **discovery, dream, and design** (emphasis mine). [Appreciative Inquiry] involves the art and practice of asking unconditionally positive questions that strengthen a system's capacity to apprehend, anticipate, and heighten positive potential. (Cooperrider and Whitney 2005)

This framework is dynamic and helps us design distinct practices with our women stakeholders with curiosity and growing interest. The approach will bring us into the actual experience of what is happening with women's philanthropic choices, rather than our stories about them. When we sincerely ask questions of ourselves and our stakeholders, we find ourselves in authentic conversations about different possibilities. We awaken our ability to connect meaningfully, to innovate and to adapt. Our partnership with women will be most successful if we engage in a curious, enlivened state to help women bring all manner of support to our missions.

This approach also fits the reality that change is hard at any time, and particularly in a fundraising environment when we are constantly in motion and trying to keep up with big goals, as well as relationships. We all strive to be effective at what we do. When we want to introduce something new, *even if we want it*, a couple of things can happen. We get a burst of energy and motivation to try a new approach. But with the slightest pressure, from within or outside ourselves, we often revert to the old "best practices." That's human nature. Or, we get energy, move forward, are successful, and then don't know what to *do* with all of the energy and change we've unleashed. If we don't build a framework to sustain the goal, our success can die off or revert to the previous status quo because there was not enough support. The Appreciative Inquiry approach can help build, individually and collectively, new skills we can employ consistently and systemic support to maintain the changes over time.

Based on the Appreciative Inquiry framework, this book is organized into four parts in which I share dozens of case studies and examples to illustrate my points.

Part I: Discover

What do we know and what do we need to know? We cannot act successfully if we remain unaware.

Chapter 1, *How Women Give,* focuses on the *facts* about women's giving based on national research. WPI has created important, grounded research on why gender matters. I include the highlights. All women do not behave the same way all the time, just as all men don't. I portray a "painting" of the differences, grounded in both research facts and in the many stories women have shared across hundreds of conversations. I also share the specific details of the extent to which women control financial decisions, both consumer and philanthropic. The goal of this section is to provide you with compelling facts about women's philanthropic power and potential and to prime your pump to grow women's philanthropy for your mission.

Chapter 2, *What Do Your Women Think?*, will help you explore your own data and interviews with women stakeholders. Listening deeply to your women stakeholders is a key part of the discovery process. How do they feel about their relationship to your organization? What are your women stakeholders saying about you? What do they care about? How can we gain more of their voice and input? What is working and what is missing? Learning to listen more openly brings deeper understanding as well as guideposts for what can be done differently.

Chapter 3, *Making Our Stories Overt,* explores current fundraising behaviors. What might be in our collective "best practices" that get in the way of growing support from women? Humans prefer certainty and patterns. How does that impede change? We may unknowingly hold myths about how women give. Becoming curious about internal narratives will awaken your energy toward change, which is a crucial ingredient to commit to new actions.

Chapter 4, *Lessons Learned,* shares the highlights from twenty-five years of learning about women's philanthropy from the field. My goal is to help you learn which advancement behaviors and choices have worked and which have not, across the many programs we have tracked. To accelerate women's philanthropy, we will do best if we build on success. With awareness about what has been learned to date, an organization can discern effective choices as it focuses on women.

Part II: Dream

This section utilizes all you've discovered to create a practical vision for what you want to accomplish as you connect with women. If discovery was enough, we'd all jump into effective action as soon as we learn new information. However, knowledge does not bring change; our behaviors do. Long-term effectiveness after the first excitement of an idea comes from gathering deeper understanding, expanding the energy to more people with different views, and clarifying what you will focus on.

Chapter 5, *Imagine,* will guide you in creating a compelling vision for building women's giving to *your* organization. What specific aspirations do you want to achieve? Changing behaviors and "best practice" processes will be awkward at best, and some will say daunting. And yet it is this very lack of adapted behaviors that has stalled the growth of women's philanthropy. I believe that only with a clear and compelling vision of the outcomes desired can we cut through the natural human resistance that occurs. With your vision, you will know when to say "no" to some ideas and actions for the sake of a clear "yes" in alignment with your goals. With your vivid, imagined picture of what is possible, you will be more likely to design and achieve bold outcomes.

Chapter 6, *Intentions,* provides examples of how you might focus your efforts with a compelling vision. The goal is to be intentional and visible with your chosen approach. Language matters. When you set a course with your intentions, and announce them publicly, the conversations and alliances that follow will be markedly different than if you simply act, alone and without a clear destination. You want to know the key strategic outcomes you are aiming for, so you can focus on designing a path to realizing those goals. Every team and organization is different, as are the women stakeholders who care about their work. Your focus will guide and drive your specific actions toward *your* goals. This section will provide examples of individual or team intentions that successfully grew women's philanthropy.

Part III: Design

This is where implementation begins, contained within a framework you chose in Part II. We can't do everything all at once. In fact, often when we embark on change, we do better to begin with a few smaller steps as we grow our new "muscles" of behavioral practice. Most of us didn't start by driving across the country when we were learning to drive!

In Part III, you will find many examples of what you might consider as you review your current practices throughout the donor cycle. Feel free to choose what matches the focus you've chosen. If it is growing the number of women in your prospect portfolios, how might adapting your research impact new ways to find, connect to and solicit women prospects? If you want to transform your communication, what language resonates? What are women looking for in your print and social media? How might you communicate to inspire women? Other examples I share include: How can you share information or involve women in meaningful ways that fit their busy lives? How do you design personal meetings? How and when do you ask for a gift and do it boldly? And is an ask always done individually, or might you include the family or network? What stewardship resonates? And finally, what are the unique metrics you want to track?

Part IV: Destiny

This section could also be called "deliver." How many times do we design new actions and engage key people, only to cut short our work when other pressures arise? Certainly, it is important to have clear actions, accountability, metrics and the engagement of the right stakeholders to keep moving forward. However, Part IV is called "destiny" because at this point in the journey you have the sustaining power of a networked team committed to your vision—continually learning, sharing, creating and collaborating. The focus on women is infused in all fundraising processes and practices and is updated whenever more is learned. Much more has occurred than the achievement of your original goal. You have created a new normal in your fundraising practices. You will not easily slide back to where you were before.

This book is designed to wake up development leaders, fundraisers and volunteers and to help them consciously create specific actions to maximize women's philanthropy. The word "consciously" is key. My goal is to make overt the hidden stories and current practices that unknowingly may not connect with women. With this awareness, you will be better able to make different choices about fundraising adaptations.

It is time to open the valve of support, power and influence of women and their philanthropy. This book is not just for the mega-gifts; there are countless women across our communities who will give to you and have not been sought out or shown the value of your cause. You can use this model to adapt behaviors that will increase the number of women meaningfully engaged in your programs, or grow supportive networks for your mission or increase bold giving to your campaign. (Once learned, you can also use the same overarching model—the four-part process of discover, dream, design, and destiny—as your guide to adapt fundraising for other donor groups.)

As seen by 19th and early 20th century movements for causes such as abolition, temperance and suffrage, women have always had an important, if not fully realized or appreciated, role to play in solving our greatest problems. Today, as hundreds of thousands of women across the political spectrum participate in marches and activism, they are signaling a clear desire to contribute to the world. Let's not miss this important moment. We have important challenges to solve in our society and women are the missing ingredient to accelerate the change we seek.

Part I

DISCOVER

Chapter 1

HOW WOMEN GIVE

Start close in,
don't take the second step
or the third,
start with the first
thing
close in,
the step
you don't want to take.
—David Whyte, "Start Close In"

Why do we need to take time to discover? You might be saying: "I know we must focus on women, so why can't we just go forward and start a women's program in our organization?"

How often have we come back from a conference very excited about something we just learned, and then failed to change our daily actions and interactions when back in the office? If we want transformational changes in our fundraising, we must look closely at what we do and its effect on others, in this case women. We need to dig deep and directly face the conundrum of not connecting successfully to our diverse donors. Why haven't we made the changes we know we need in our sector after all these years? What stands in the way?

I like Brené Brown's approach. In her book, *Rising Strong*, she writes that we need to "rumble" with our stories to find the truth (Brown 2015, 52–53). She asks, "How do we come to those *aha* moments if we are not willing to explore and ask questions?" Her choice of the word "rumble" evokes great visuals for me—grappling, on the floor, getting messy, untangling knots or piles of stuff.

It is time to rumble with our stories about women's philanthropy. Rumbling begins with deep inquiry, shirt sleeves rolled up, shoulder to shoulder with colleagues and straight talk about what we know or don't know and what barriers might be getting in the way of raising more money from women.

Humans, and the systems they create, grow in the direction they focus their attention and questions. Curiosity is a great starting point. Curiosity can help unlock assumptions that are often unconscious and unspoken. Curiosity has a naturally wider lens of seeing and hearing. It can open our eyes to practices we've not analyzed and input we've not taken time to consider.

As we engage in discovery, new questions arise that will inform us about our assumptions, fundraising practices and organizational structures that may be impeding women from donating to our organizations. We will also hear stories and open ourselves up to possibilities we may not have considered. The *appreciative inquiry* framework, starting with discovery, allows us to move beyond the traditional focus of correcting problems, such as the question of how we grow more revenue for our missions. In their introductory book on Appreciative Inquiry, David Cooperrider and Diana Whitney write:

> Are you tired of the same old discussions of what's not working, how hard it is to overcome, and who's to blame? Do you have hopes and dreams for your organization? Would you like to see engagement, commitment, and enthusiasm rise along with revenues? (Cooperrider and Whitney 2005, 6)

After 20 years of being involved with women's philanthropy, I can assure you that when you deepen your curiosity about how women give, you have a higher likelihood of gaining engagement, commitment and financial support from this important group of supporters.

Your Discovery Team

Before you start with discovery, engage a few partners or a team. As you'll read later, too many initiatives in the past 25 years struggled because they were run by a single, isolated person, sometimes working part-time, who lacked strong backing from their organization. There is power in engaging team members and stakeholders to help grapple with the information you learn. Having support for the effort from a decision maker is also critical.

I've seen several variations of organizational teams that work together to learn about and grow women's philanthropy for their mission. The most successful have been time-bound task forces that were made up of a few staff members plus several volunteers and donors (women primarily, but some included men). The group had direct access to leadership decision making. In other words, there was an organizational commitment for this inquiry, a significant leader signed off on the effort and the voices and input of volunteers were heard as discoveries were unearthed.

This team approach allows your stakeholders and leadership to help guide the strategy, provide input on the process and data and be part of designing the initiatives that best fit your organization. As Melissa Effron Hayek, director of women and philanthropy at the University of California, Los Angeles, shared with me:

> We knew what we wanted to do as staff; some wanted to just get started. I knew there was a better way. We engaged a group of women donors and development department stakeholders. As they worked together with us through the process, we found that they created even more substantial change than we had imagined. The program is much stronger thanks to their involvement.

As you'll read throughout this book, the voices of women donors and stakeholders is paramount to design a program that takes you beyond your imagination. The idea of a task force made up of diverse, thoughtful individuals to explore new opportunities is an action you likely have taken with other endeavors, based on a compelling reason. With the persuasive research on women's economic power and philanthropic influence, you can craft a strong argument for why it is time for your organization to focus on support from women. Here is one compelling case, which led to formal support for the organization's effort:

> We propose a collaborative effort between Principal Gifts and Major Gifts to create a formal structure focused on women's leadership giving. Our earlier report suggested a gender gap in engagement with and giving to [our organization]. With this first major campaign since that report was issued, and with several prime factors in place to improve our fundraising tradition, [our organization] must prepare itself both to capitalize on the wealth generated and inherited by its alumnae, and to capture the leadership potential of alumnae newly stepping forward with significant financial support. [Our] initiative has the potential to be a game-changing component [for our organization].

The task force created by this team reviewed the research and literature, listened to the results of a survey and focus groups and dug deeply into the organizational data. They reported their draft strategy back to the leadership, which approved it. Five years later, the resulting effort is raising significant new financial support and increased leadership from women.

Let's Start With the Research

Women in the Global Economy

A thought-provoking article was written in late 2017: "The Silent Rise of the Female-Driven Economy." It noted:

> Women are the single largest productive economic force and drive almost every economic indicator for businesses. But that's not the impression we get when we read economic data or view advertising.
>
> According to some estimates, women control *85% of consumer spending in the U.S.* Why? Because your average woman makes purchases for herself, her husband or partner, her children and also her elderly parents. Women make 70% of major financial decisions for themselves and their families, everything from auto, home, and investment. Globally, women control *$36 trillion in total wealth.*
>
> Based on statistics released in 2015, women collectively represent *the second largest economy in the world* based on earned income vs GDP. This would seem like a logical assumption because women make up half the population, but due to a lack of data, this number *undercounts female contribution to the global economy.* These numbers don't account for the fact that women are paid 25–40% less than men globally, and that your average woman does an estimated 4.5 hours of unpaid work daily (22.5 hours per week). (Kayembe 2017)

Let's take this global lens and narrow its focus to the United States.

Women's Economic Power

The Women's Philanthropy Institute is the global leader for research on women's philanthropy. WPI increases understanding of women's philanthropy through rigorous research and education, interpreting and broadly sharing these insights to improve philanthropy. With a constellation of evidence on dozens of topics, WPI is the key hub for understanding with certainty how women approach giving.

WPI offers an overarching context for women's philanthropy in its 2015 literature review, *How and Why Women Give*:

> Women have been active in philanthropy in the United States throughout its history, but women today have the potential to take an increased role in philanthropy. Over the past 40 years, women's roles have changed dramatically in American society as they have made significant gains in their progress toward economic and social equality with men. With increasing incomes, educational attainment, and control over wealth, women have never had so much control over philanthropic resources. (Mesch et al. 2015a, 3)

The demographic changes referred to are impressive when taken together:

- Many women are not marrying. There are almost three times as many female single-headed households as male households (15.3 million versus 5.8 million) (Lofquist et al. 2012, 4).
- Women are marrying later and having fewer children, which translates into married women having more disposable income (Vespa 2017, 5, 10).
- Women are earning more educational degrees. They are now the majority in undergraduate settings and comprise more than half of all university and college alumni. With increased education comes increased earnings (Bureau of Labor Statistics 2011).
- The traditional breadwinner-homemaker model of the American family no longer dominates; over half of women in married couple households are employed. In 40 percent of households, women are *the primary* breadwinners (Wang, Parker and Taylor 2013).
- Two of every five businesses in the country—more than 10 million enterprises—are owned by women. Their combined wealth is estimated to be more than $6 trillion (Swank 2010, 45).
- More women are in professional positions generating higher incomes.
  - Women hold 51 percent of managerial and professional jobs in the workforce (Bureau of Labor Statistics 2014, 2).
  - Of the top wealth holders in the U.S., 42 percent are women, including more that 3 million with annual incomes greater than $550,000 (IRS 2007).

- Women are the fastest growing segment of wealthy individuals; in the past decade, the number of women earning more than $100,000 has tripled (Witter and Chen 2008, 14).
- Women are strong investors. They tend to have a more disciplined approach to investing that contributes to higher risk-adjusted returns compared with men (Wells Fargo 2017, 7).

This economic shift adds up to women controlling significant wealth. From a recent report by WPI:

> While exact figures are difficult to pin down, media reports estimate that women control up to 60% of wealth in the U.S. ($10 trillion–$12 trillion in 2008), which is projected to grow to up to $22 trillion by 2020 . . . When coupled with the trillions of dollars anticipated in the inter-generational wealth transfers of the coming decades, women may have access to previously unimaginable resources for the common good. (Mesch et al. 2015a, 41)

Women's Philanthropic Influence

With increased earnings and education, women have demonstrated an increased focus on philanthropy. Women are giving more and influencing more philanthropy. Repeatedly, studies find that women have a greater inclination to giving than men:

- Single women are *more likely* than similarly-situated single men to give to charity (Mesch 2010a, 6).
- Women *give significantly more* than similarly-situated men at almost all income levels (Ibid).
- Baby boomers and older women are more likely to give than their male counterparts at all giving levels (Mesch et al. 2015a, 25).
- Women are *more likely to give more* to 10 out of 11 charitable subsectors, with the exception of the sports/recreation subsector (O'Connor et al. 2018, 3).

Women's philanthropic influence becomes all the more apparent when we understand household giving patterns.

- For every $10,000 that the wife's income increases, total household giving increases by more than 5 percent. In comparison, for every $10,000 the husband's income increases, total household giving increases by 3 percent (Mesch 2016).

- WPI found that nearly three-quarters of general population households decide jointly on philanthropy and, in high-net-worth households, nearly half jointly decide. When only one spouse decides, the wife decides twice as often as the husband. This means that the women of the household are almost always involved in the family gift decision (Center on Philanthropy 2011, 7; Lenok 2016).
- Women's influence in giving decisions transcends generations. One WPI study examined whether generational shifts in charitable giving intersect with women's changing decision-making roles within families. The researchers looked at people from two different generations while each were ages 25–47 to better understand generational shifts in charitable behavior. For GenX/millennial married couples whose giving decisions were influenced by women, the estimate of the amount of giving is higher than that of their pre-Boomer counterparts. For GenX/millennial married couples whose giving decisions are made by men only, the estimate of giving is lower than that of their pre-baby-boom counterparts (Mesch et al. 2016, 16).

The bottom line is that women's influence in charitable giving is on the rise—and the dollars are following. Women are prone to give more.

Consider: Given the above research, do you track single women? Do you ask directly about how philanthropic decisions are made in the household? Have you considered cultivating both baby boomer and millennial women in the same household, or bringing the two generations together in equal numbers when designing a task force or asking for input?

Women's Giving Capacity

Although women might not yet be known for mega-gifts, they can—and do— give big.

- The Million Dollar List compiled by the IUPUI Lilly Family School of Philanthropy shows that between 2000 and 2013, 815 women made gifts of $1 million or more. And the emphasis is on "or more," as their total giving amounted to $4,594,010,000.
- Women Moving Millions, a nonprofit that started in 2007, raises million-dollar gifts from women for causes that support women and girls. The initial campaign raised over $182 million from 102 women over a three-year period, well exceeding its goal of $150 million. As of 2017, this

community of donors has grown to 282 individuals who have given or pledged at least $1 million or more to organizations of their choice that primarily serve women and girls.

- Women are notable in the list of 154 members of the Giving Pledge. Focused on billionaires, the Giving Pledge encourages the world's wealthiest individuals and families to donate much of their wealth to philanthropic causes. Many women members have earned their own wealth (Sara Blakely, founder of Spanx, is one example among many others) or are influential in directing wealth shared with their spouses in making this philanthropic pledge.

- Preeti Gill (2018), founder of Sole Searcher Strategies, a prospect development consultancy in Vancouver, Canada, keeps a public list called, "Donations at the Diva Level." She wrote about outright or bequest mega-gifts from women in 2017, totaling over $135 million. While this list is not comprehensive because it's based on public press releases that Gill finds, it is impressive. Here are two stories that Gill reports:
  - Phyllis Hanse was a former piano teacher. She left a $4.2 million estate to a number of charities that help children, high school students, a local church and the library in Webster, South Dakota.
  - Stacy Smith Branca is from Dartmouth's Class of 1994. Still in her 40s, she and her family made a $2 million gift to endow the women's soccer head coach position.

Consider: Are you bold in the asks of women? Are you overlooking women (and men) who could give $1 million or $4 million because you see headlines of mega-giving at $25 million, $100 million and more? Gill calls this "donation desensitization," when fundraisers who track giving trends closely become so focused on leaps in the sizes of mega-gifts that they lose sight of smaller but still significant donation possibilities.

Women's Giving Behavior

While women focus on philanthropy more than men and make big gifts, they give in different ways.

Women tend to *spread their giving across more organizations*, while men concentrate their giving. While not true of all women, there are many who give to a wide range of organizations in smaller amounts.

Consider: How does the fact that women spread their giving impact your research approach? Are you able to find, or inquire about, the aggregate giving a woman is making? Do you ask directly where her recent gift to you fits in with all her other philanthropic commitments? If you knew the aggregate amount she has given, how might that affect your rating for a potential ask?

Gender differences do emerge in motivations for giving among high-net-worth men and women. Women's top motivations are similar to men's:

- Belief that their gift can make a difference,
- Sense of personal satisfaction from giving,
- Loyalty to the same causes each year, and
- Desire to give back to their community.

However, women more than men give when: a) it aligns with their values, b) they are engaged (volunteering, on a task force or board) and c) something unexpected arises such as disasters or a short-term challenge. For instance, women are more likely than men to give on #Giving Tuesday (Mesch 2010b, 4–5; Osili et al. 2017, 4).

Here is an excerpt from WPI's literature review on *Where Do Men and Women Give?*

> Our findings on donor motivations reveal new information on how to better engage women in nonprofit organizations. Women report that they are motivated to give because they are on the board or volunteer for an organization, a finding that is not salient for men. As a result, nonprofits would be well-served to continue to diversify their boards and offer women meaningful volunteer roles to increase their participation. Women report needing first-hand involvement to increase their motivations to give. Fundraisers should keep this in mind prior to soliciting women for a charitable donation. (Mesch et al. 2015b, 30)

Consider: How often do you ask about a woman's motivations and your organization's fit with her values during a first visit? Have you ever asked her to tell the story of her philanthropy—with any organization? You will learn a lot about motivation, preferred engagement, stewardship and her values as she tells that story.

Many women are more inclined to work with others when supporting a cause. WPI's 2017 Symposium highlighted the power of women collaborating to create powerful philanthropy. The Symposium started with opening remarks by Melinda Gates, co-chair and trustee of the Bill & Melinda Gates Foundation:

This is our strength as women—we cooperate, we collaborate and we innovate to amplify our voices and accelerate change.

As natural netweavers, women prefer to connect with others to create impact together. Yes, I wrote net*weavers*, not networkers. While networking is used to make connections that may help you in your career or with a business idea you have, netweaving takes those connections to a deeper level. The phrase was coined by Bob Littell over 15 years ago. Littell is now chief netweaver at Netweaver International in Atlanta. He notes:

When people are networking, it's really about "How can you help me?" and "Can you give me something I need?" With netweaving, it's all about "How I can help you?" and "Is there someone I know who would benefit from meeting you?" (Strang 2011)

This approach can build trusted relationships, and women are attentive to building relationships. When they gather, they share information about their worlds, personal and professional. They offer connections and ideas to each other and join in action. Philanthropic networks are popular with women because they create a connection to the group and open the way for collective impact on a specific cause.

The preference of many women to collaborate rather than be individual philanthropists is an important distinction, especially as today's fundraising practices more often focus on individual strategies.

Consider: How often do you invite a woman to a cultivation event and encourage her to bring someone from her network? Or make it easy for her to share what she just learned with her network? Do you purposely design collective solicitation strategies for groups of women of capacity, as well as individual strategies for each? When you host an event, do you provide time for women to netweave with each other? Later in the book, you will read about successful outcomes from organizations who have approached the network, not just the individual.

Women expect to be engaged with and understand an organization before they are asked for a gift. For some women, that might take a single conversation, particularly if they are asked about their values or for their input. Others might prefer to give their time or expertise for a period of time before giving. Approaching these women first for a gift can make them feel rushed and unappreciated. Below is a summary of consistent themes from one nonprofit after interviewing their women stakeholders:

- Compelling reasons to support XX organization?
  - Believe in mission and reputation
- Thoughts on philanthropy?
  - Must know and see the need before they give
  - Want to understand the impact and how their gift will be used
- Thoughts on engagement?
  - Want opportunities for active engagement
  - Inspired by XX organization's stories but "want to be involved beyond just giving"
- Thoughts on leadership?
  - Want to be involved, but unsure if the organization needs or wants their input

These responses are like hundreds of others I have heard in focus groups and surveys.

Consider: When you rate a woman prospect's capacity to make a gift, do you also rate the level of engagement, understanding and trust she has in you? Do you design at least two visits or interactions before a solicitation so you can learn what she has to offer beyond money? Are you authentic in asking for input when it is appropriate and sharing the impact of her support, whether it comes in the form of time, talent or treasure?

Women may take longer than men to make decisions about gift giving or other forms of engagement. There is a lot of research on the fact that women consider a myriad of factors when choosing their next car, family vacations or simply coordinating the family calendar.

A recent Wells Fargo Investment Institute report on women and investing found that women are more likely than men to seek education and advice from investment professionals, and that this is a benefit. "Women's greater willingness to show patience, forgo excessive trading, seek education and adhere to an investment plan has tended to result in better investment results . . . These traits lead them to perform better than men as investors" (Wells Fargo 2017, 9).

In philanthropy, as in investment, women want to understand, check facts and be involved to make sure they are making a trustworthy choice with their gift. And they want to know, up front, the likely impact.

Consider: If you reframe engagement for women as part of due diligence, what different questions might you ask her along the path of connecting to your organization? How might engagement opportunities be designed to grow her passion for the mission as well as meet her desire for specific facts? Fundraisers value retention of donors, because it's more cost effective to keep a donor than find new ones. How do we measure the cost of some engagement or information shared with a woman who cares enough to come forward versus costly donor acquisition for new prospects?

Women might unconsciously look for high-impact volunteer work over high-profile roles. The placement of women on your boards and councils may be a crucial step to grow their philanthropy. I first heard about this concept in 2013 from Nannerl O. Keohane, former president of Duke University and Wellesley College. While speaking to a task force of women from Duke, she noted that young women are often socialized to behave differently than men regarding leadership. They will choose roles where they can work with others to make change, rather than seek for themselves a high-profile role with a title such as board chair or council president. This generalization certainly does not apply to all women and, even as I write, more women are assuming leadership roles and making tough decisions. However, it is important to be aware of how this deep socialization may unconsciously impact your leadership-prospect pool of both women and men. You may not "see" as many women waving their hands to be groomed to help lead your organization.

Consider: You may need to educate a woman you are considering for leadership on the importance of stepping into a high-profile role because it can extend her desired impact. Also consider how you might track women across the years. Women zig zag in their careers as they navigate family commitments and other personal life changes. Their attention to your mission may vary over time. How are you staying in touch so they think of your organization when they ARE ready for leadership roles?

Why Bother?

Women's giving behavior is the most important differentiator for fundraisers to understand and adapt their own behaviors to match. However, in reading this section, one might still ask "Why should I? Working with women takes too long." If the economic reasons are not convincing enough, consider two additional reasons laid out well by Lisa Witter and Lisa Chen in *The She Spot: Why Women Are the Market for Changing the World—And How to Reach Them*.

When you gain a woman's trust in your organization, her loyalty keeps her close to your mission AND she brings her network with her. "When you market well to women, you benefit from the world's most powerful marketing tool: word of mouth . . . Women who are true believers can help make believers of others by spreading the good word to friends and family or by simply giving their honest appraisal of why they're . . . supporting an issue," according to Witter and Chen (2008, 16). This translates into building your donor pipeline quickly with other donors who also will bring their networks. The results are exponential in giving and networking, vs. one gift at a time.

Moreover, when you meet women's high standards, you are also meeting the demands of the men on your donor list. These days, more and more donors consider themselves "investors." While men may not ask all the upfront questions women do, they ask questions in different ways at different times in the relationship. I've always remembered my mentor Martha Taylor's quote: "When you approach women like men, you lose the women. When you approach women as they prefer, you get the women AND the men." And given that women make or influence most philanthropic decisions in households, this should be considered a basic rule for all donor strategies.

Chapter 2

WHAT DO YOUR WOMEN THINK?

"The future is brought into the present when citizens engage each other through questions of possibility, commitment, dissent and gifts."
—Peter Block, *Community: The Structure of Belonging*

This chapter will help you gain awareness of what might be right under your nose. What is the baseline information about how women are currently giving to you? What do your women stakeholders think about you? Why do they care about you? What do they have to say about their philanthropy? What are your organization's strengths and values?

We know from a large body of research that working from an organization's strengths to achieve change has a higher success rate than focusing on gaps and problems. Peter Drucker, a highly regarded leader of change management, once noted in an interview: "The task of organizational leadership is to create an alignment of strengths in ways that make the system's weaknesses irrelevant" (Cook 2013).

Leadership Data

How do women, imagining themselves as connected with your organization through their giving, see a reflection of themselves, or not, in your organizational leadership? People often start researching an organization by looking at leadership—the names and photos of those who are part of decision-making. They make strong impressions from images and names, without ever reading the bios. If women philanthropists see only a few female leaders, or don't see any, they may conclude that your organization is not a good fit for them.

Gender diversity on boards is important. There is growing evidence that a company's bottom line increases when women are part of the decision-making. A study published in the 2013 *International Journal of Business Governance and Ethics* found that women take the interests of multiple stakeholders in account to arrive at fair and moral decisions. This translates into better performance for their companies. Boards with high female representation experience a 53 percent higher return on equity (Carter and Wagner 2011).

Despite the evidence, the United States is far behind other countries in the number of women on boards. Fortunately, attention and intention can help create change. The Thirty Percent Coalition, formed in 2011 as a collaboration of investors, corporations and public sector leaders, uses the collective clout of its 80-plus members and their diversity to increase the number of women appointed to boards. As of October 2016, more than 100 targeted companies had elected new women to their boards.

Such intention is warranted at many nonprofits and universities. When Duke University reviewed the number of women on its many boards in 2013, they found they had an average of 24 percent of women across 11 primary boards. Some had a high proportion of women because they were primarily "women's boards," such as the Nursing Advisory Board with women making up 71 percent of the board membership. The least diverse boards were those that had predominantly male student and alumni populations until fairly recently, such as schools of medicine at 18 percent, business at just 11 percent and engineering at 13 percent. This same inequity was true at the College of William & Mary. Despite having the name William & Mary, the gender makeup across all boards in 2013 was 63 percent men and 37 percent women. The proportion of women leaders at both universities did not reflect the percentage of women students or alumnae, at more than half and just over 50 percent respectively.

Donor Data

Analysis of your donor database or constituent-management system will uncover the current story of women giving to your institution. I know that many of you might be reeling at this suggestion, ready to complain about your system. Indeed, I recognize that the way many systems are constructed creates headaches when you try to analyze giving by gender. Without clear processes or procedures, there may be inaccurate entries about a gift from a household, even if there is clear evidence that the woman made, or was a key part of, the decision. I have no doubt that the overwhelming evidence of women's philanthropic influence requires an overhaul of many well-known constituent-management systems. I hope plans for these changes are in the works.

In the meantime, even basic analysis on current giving by gender will help you uncover new information.

The leaders of an environmental organization began reviewing how their women donors gave. They started by analyzing the organization's direct-mail program. They found that women were making 51 percent of the gifts and men 49 percent, which underscored their mission's resonance with women. However, the men's average size gift was larger, and the comparison of men and women giving more than $1,000 was significant: 962 men gave over $1,000, compared to 653 women.

McGill University found that its traditional comparison of average size gifts, $76 for men and $64 for women, did not tell the whole story. The university looked more deeply at generational trends and found that while women were giving less than men across all generations, women who had graduated in the year 2000 or later were giving more than men.

Duke University analyzed average lifetime giving by undergraduate degree alumni and found a significant discrepancy between men and women, with alumnae giving $7,857, less than half of alumni at $19,085. The school did further analysis of giving against capacity, defined as an individual's ability to make a five-year gift to charity, and found that women giving $25,000 or more were giving at a lower percentage than men with the same capacity.

To use your donor data to tell a powerful story, I highly recommend framing your findings as "missed income right now." Many of us have learned from sales people that saying, "you could be making $10 million more a year" is less persuasive than saying "you've been losing $10 million a year for the past few years." When William & Mary did an analysis of 2015 donations, it found that if the average gift women gave was the same as men, it would have raised an extra $3.4 million that year.

There are many ways to look at your data—from the traditional gender difference in average size gifts at various levels, to the analysis of participation in engagement activities, to understanding the gender difference in donors' lifetime giving values. These tell you what is happening right now. Further analysis of historical perspectives, demographics and emerging trends, such as McGill's review of generational trends, can help you consider where you might focus your efforts. In addition, your data will likely prompt more questions. All three of these organizations used the data they found to create questions to ask their women donors and learn what factors drove the differences in giving.

If you are part of a girl's school or college, or a nonprofit focused on women and girls, you might assume that your women stakeholders and prospects see themselves in your public face. Women might make up most of your board, you mainly visit women, you have predominantly women in your constituent-management system and you tell stories about the girls or young women you serve. I still encourage you to analyze your donors. You might find unexpected groupings of donors to learn more about, or you can ask your donors why they give and how their giving to you compares with the other organizations they support. Learning about their giving behavior can open up new conversations and potential opportunities for funding.

Know Your Donors and Stakeholders

I can't emphasize enough how important it is to get the actual perceptions of women donors and other stakeholders into your discovery process before you move forward into vision and design. Surveys, focus groups and structured interviews can provide critical information about women donors and stakeholders such as board members, leadership and development staff. However, when not done correctly, such explorations can lead to mistaken findings and bad decisions. When done well, you gain invaluable information, so it helps to work with someone who can design your psychometrics.

Asking questions of women can provide rich, qualitative information. And as you know, asking questions is a wonderful cultivation technique for donors and prospects. When we listen to others and open our own thinking, we end up testing our conscious or unconscious assumptions. Asking high-quality questions and really paying attention to the answers helps update beliefs. It also develops a shared understanding of differences that leads to better decisions. Inquiry from a position of curiosity and openness to absorb new information not only reveals the strengths of your organization. It also uncovers how your women stakeholders see you and how they see themselves connecting with your organization now and in the future. Asking questions also builds relationships, enabling people to be understood as human beings rather than in their "roles" of leader, staff member or donor. As we all know, building authentic relationships is at the core of our fundraising.

Bring the voice of your women stakeholders into your discovery. Asking a woman one-on-one about her experiences in philanthropy will provide you with rich, qualitative answers not gathered in larger groups or surveys. If you have limited time, pose the following questions to several of your donors:

- Describe your most exciting experience in giving to date. It does not need to be related to this organization.
  - Tell the story. What happened?
  - What enabled this gift? What role did you play? What role did the organization play? What role did the staff person play in relationship to this experience?
  - What else made this experience possible?

You will learn her values, motivations and preferences for relationships, information and stewardship.

Here is an example of one women's memorable story:

I made my gift because I was asked. Of course, it wasn't as simple as that, but it was key. I lead with this because there was a nonprofit in my town that I cared deeply about. They knew me personally, my daughter was engaged in their work, they asked my advice at times, but they never asked me for a gift. For that reason, I did not give to them. Well, I did make a few small gifts, but definitely not what I could have.

In contrast, this one organization really went out of its way to get to know me. They not only asked me for advice at times, but they got to know my family and what I cared about. They always made a point of asking about my family and what I was up to before talking about their latest activities. When I made a first gift of about $500 they did great stewardship. It was for a scholarship, and I was only one of many supporting the scholarship. It is not that I did it all myself. Yet I still received a hand-written note from one of the students. And I was invited to an event with their leaders. I couldn't go, but I felt included. They continued to update me on their work. I think I got something in writing or a call every quarter about the latest initiatives and their impact. I liked it when they shared their progress on an evaluation system for their work.

Last fall, they scheduled a call with me and my husband. (He is also interested in the work, although less involved.) We, of course, knew that this meant we would be asked for a gift. The CEO led the call and did not start with anything about the organization. She asked how we were, and what was holding our attention at that time. We felt her true interest in what we shared.

Then she described a very poignant need and made a big ask of us, noting we'd be leaders of this initiative. It was more than we had expected, but with a couple of conversations, we figured out a way to do it. It has been so rewarding to see the new initiative unfold and know we were part of helping create this change.

This donor shared what resonated with her. Being asked for a gift was not the only thing that was important. She also appreciated the personal conversation as well as being valued beyond what she might give. She was paying attention to how she was stewarded and the impact of the organization's work. Finally, she felt respected when she and her husband were asked to be among the leaders for a new initiative. She was thrilled to help make change possible.

After you hear these stories from several of your top donors, you may begin to hear themes. One organization really deepened understanding of their women donors when they reviewed key themes about what motivated giving:

- Pride in the organization
- Deep involvement
- Creating change for the future
- Opening opportunities for self and others
- Inclusive
- Using my voice
- Inspired by the organization
- Connected to the community
- Practical application to the real world

When these themes were prioritized, the top four were:

- Inclusive
- Practical
- Opening opportunities
- Connected to the real world

This organization would never have gained a sense of these top motivations from the giving records in the database. They provided a rich framework for deeper inquiry and ultimately the design of their plan to connect to women.

Gathering Your Stakeholder Input

Assessment processes to gain stakeholders' input vary with each organization based on size and budget, but generally mean listening to a cross section of your staff and donors and volunteers. Some organizations do one-on-one interviews. Others combine personal interviews with small focus groups. Others also add, or only do, broad surveys.

It is important to consider up-front whom to survey in your organization, how the outreach will occur, who will conduct the interviews, who will analyze the data and how the stories, quotes and trends that are revealed will be communicated. There is also an opportunity, with permission, to capture the stories and write them up for your newsletter or website.

Below is one chart showing sample categories of questions that might be asked. You can turn to experts in your organization, within your volunteer base or beyond, to help you create the assessment methodology and questions, and then analyze the results. The power is in probing for what works, what can be appreciated and furthered. The goal is not to search for what is wrong, but to get inspired by what is already happening that can be valued and expanded.

	Staff Interviews	Stakeholder Interviews	Large Group Survey
Experience with and General Impressions of XX Organization			
Perception of XX Organization	✓	✓	✓
Knowledge about XX Organization	✓	✓	✓
Communication from XX Organization		✓	✓
Organizational strengths and values	✓	✓	
Engagement			
Level of engagement with XX Organization		✓	✓
Means of engagement		✓	✓
Motivations for engagement		✓	✓
Knowledge about XX Organization's volunteer leadership	✓	✓	
Role as a volunteer leader at XX Organization		✓	

	Staff Interviews	Stakeholder Interviews	Large Group Survey
Leadership			
Suggestions for increasing women's leadership at XX Organization	✓	✓	
Philanthropy			
Personal philanthropic decision making		✓	✓
Tell your philanthropic high-point experience		✓	
Number of organizations supported		✓	✓
Determining factors for gift size		✓	✓
Motivations for increasing gift size		✓	✓
Culture of philanthropy at XX Organization	✓		
Motivations for giving/not giving to XX Organization		✓	✓
Suggestions for increasing women's giving to XX Organization	✓	✓	✓
Women's Philanthropy (WP)			
Impression of the need and potential benefits of intentional focus on women		✓	✓
Changes required at XX Organization to grow WP	✓	✓	
Current programs at XX Organization that compete with/complement this focus	✓		
Suggestions/best practices for success with WP	✓	✓	
Key messages for women donors/partners		✓	
Interest in participation		✓	✓
Suggestions for stakeholders to become involved	✓		
Other			
Demographic data			✓

Note that this chart includes staff interviews. Staff can share stories about mistakes made in cultivating women, as well as successes. They can open up about lessons learned. As insiders, they can share insights about current culture, unique moments in time, strengths and values of the organization and suggestions to consider.

The summary of all the answers from interviews, focus groups or surveys can reveal important information you may not have known. Below are examples of unexpected information from two different organizations.

One university did an online survey of 4,400 alumnae with an identified high capacity to give $25,000 or more. Two unique findings were:

- Alumnae supported educational institutions as a priority, AND other educational institutions at the higher and secondary education levels were the strongest competition for alumnae philanthropic dollars.
- Alumnae perceived engagement as a prerequisite to giving to that university. Yet the data showed a relatively weak link between a donor's engagement and subsequent giving. The university learned it would need to make the link more explicitly.

Another university did both one-on-one interviews and a survey and had findings different from those above:

- There was not much of a link between being a student leader on campus and later philanthropy.
  - However, there was a stronger correlation when the women had led projects at work. A majority of these women were also strong annual donors.
- Engagement with the university through participation in on-campus or off-campus events strongly correlated with giving to the university.
  - Attendance at events correlated as much to increased giving as longer-term engagement vehicles, such as serving on committees.

The analysis of your data will be unique to your organization, culture and the experiences of your stakeholders. You will have quantitative data you might never have gathered or understood before. Furthermore, qualitative data will produce stories and quotations and reveal longings. The voices of your stakeholders will be a strong tool to cut through myths and generate potential ideas to pursue. The voice of the staff will reveal what strengths or opportunities can be developed. The results will lead you to engage in deeper levels of conversation, learning and exploration. This data will help create a foundation for your design of specific new behaviors to maximize women's philanthropy.

Chapter 3

MAKING OUR STORIES OVERT

"The third agreement is Don't Make Assumptions. *We have the tendency to make assumptions about everything. The problem with assumptions is that we believe they are the truth. We could swear they are real."*
—Don Miguel Ruiz, *The Four Agreements*

In this chapter, I move from the donors to the fundraisers. I also move from specific facts about how women give to the various beliefs we *might* hold about women's philanthropy. It is important to look directly at the stories we carry, for they form our view of life and the actions we subsequently take— often unconsciously.

Sometimes, stories we hold about ourselves come from having made an assumption at some point. Assumptions refer to the beliefs, opinions and interpretations we hold. But too often we don't view an assumption as a set of opinions. We take it as a fact. An assumption, unexamined, holds us within the world that it creates.

I worked with a talented woman I'll call "Mary." She was a fundraiser for a small nonprofit serving young women in college. She was very personable and a great story teller. In addition, she was a whiz at numbers and could create donor analytics and budgets with ease. When I started working with Mary, she made it clear that she could not write. She based that opinion on how long it took her to produce any written document. Writing was agony for her, so she designed her days to focus on the numbers of fundraising as well as the personal relationships with her staff and donors. She avoided writing documents and reports about impact or opportunities.

Mary shared with me one day that she was stressed because she needed to make a case for a campaign—in writing. No one else could do it. When we examined her assumption about writing, we found she believed that the writing task was done with pen and paper in a quiet space with no interruptions. That certainly did not describe her busy office or home! She also found writing to be isolating and boring. When I asked her to think creatively about how she might communicate a compelling case for the campaign to her team and donors, she hit on the possibility of capturing her stories and ideas with technology that translates the spoken word into writing. With that shift in thinking, Mary produced a compelling written argument in short order. Only then did she realize that her assumption that she was not a writer was based on her belief that there was only one way to write.

Beliefs or assumptions often influence the way we approach the future. For instance, I believe that my colleague, Sarah, is competent to run an upcoming and likely challenging board meeting. I ground my assumption with facts because I saw her competently lead a complex team project the previous month. I declare my decision publicly. I tell all stakeholders that Sarah is in charge of the meeting. People start organizing around Sarah as they prepare for the meeting. She creates a strong agenda and asks the team to analyze the facts. The board chair looks to her for ideas. This is an influencing story. My grounded, fact-based assessment changed Sarah's assumption of her own competence and also changed assumptions others held about her. The goal is to challenge our assumptions to be able to make grounded assessments.

Problems can arise when we forget that any assessment is still only a probability. An assessment is better than an assumption, but it is not 100 percent certain that Sarah will be the right person to facilitate the difficult board conversations. The information I used from the past may not necessarily work in the future. Believing that even assessments are infallible limits us from change. When we are willing to look at our stories, assumptions or assessments and stay open to reevaluation, we take powerful steps toward change. What are our stories, assumptions or assessments about women's philanthropy?

Best Practices?

I'll start with the collective unconscious story about our fundraising best practices. If we call them "best" practices, then that must be what they are. We should always aim to use them, correct? Let's look at this story. Where did the best practices come from?

The roots of modern U.S. philanthropy "best practices" started growing in the 1960s when the prototypical donor was a white, straight male. We tried different strategies to gain his support. Strategies we found to work were shared and replicated. These included competition, deadlines, recognition, board positions and peer pressure to raise funds.

The predominant organizations fundraising at that time were universities. As they gained confidence in how to raise money from men, many universities began organizing and professionalizing the work. Rules, systems and staffing structures were put in place to solidify the fundraising profession and more consistently meet the growing financial needs on campuses. The strategies that worked became part of staff training:

"This is how you ask for an annual gift."

"Here is an often-successful approach for inviting him to join our board."

"If you want a major gift, make sure to note who else is giving what."

"Competition and recognition work; identify who wants to lead the campaign and give the top gift."

The ways to gain support from white males continued to be replicated, extending out further to many fundraisers. These "best practices" were shared across campuses, further normalizing fundraising. At some point, the university best practices were embraced by nonprofits as well, shared by consultants as well as staff that moved from universities to nonprofits.

Almost 60 years later, many annual appeals still start with, "Please give before June 30." Levels of giving to be part of a "giving society" are often created with a focus on name recognition and access to leaders. An individual ask often includes a mention of what another person or group has given and the desire to surpass that level. Campaigns start setting goals from the top down. Galas often have a short and intense "pledge your gift now" segment during which individuals quickly raise their hands or paddles to give, urged on by the pressure of the time constraint and what others are pledging. These approaches work well—but only for a portion of our donor base.

We've made a factual assessment that we have fundraising best practices, and have forgotten that they were designed for the donor pool of the 1950s and 1960s. If we face this fact, then our curiosity awakens. The past is not necessarily prologue for how we need to fundraise in the future. Our interest is piqued to learn when these practices work for women, when they do not and why.

Fundraising Best Practices Can Impede Adaptation

Can't we just "wake up" and adapt what we are doing to connect to women? We can and need to adapt, but we need to rumble first with how deep and integrated—and mainly unconscious—these best practices are for us. It is hard to simply break free without becoming more aware of the hundreds of processes these practices have generated.

All the ways we learned to raise money from primarily men went beyond simple replication. They became codified functional skills required in our profession. Every person who wanted to learn how to fundraise practiced these skills over and over. When we practice anything over and over, the skills move from the foreground of our consciousness to the background because we've made them part of who we are. In our profession, we *become* an annual fundraiser, or a planned giving officer or a researcher. We are what we practice; we have embodied our work.

There is a lot of solid research on neuroscience regarding how the brain is designed to recognize patterns and replicate them, so we can function without having to think through every step. For example, how do you put on winter clothes when it is cold outside? You know immediately how to get into your coat, zip it, and then put on a hat, gloves, boots and scarf to protect yourself, all while talking to your loved ones and deciding on the restaurant for that evening. Your conversation is totally unrelated to your actions, which you do unconsciously. It wasn't always this way. As a child, you needed to learn each step, and it was hard. You did not get your feet into the boots easily, nor could you pull up the zipper. Every parent recognizes the time it takes to help children learn how to dress themselves. But all that practice years ago was encoded in neural patterns. Now when you want to go outside in the winter, you unconsciously hit "play" for the right neural pattern, and voilà, it's done.

In fundraising, replicating patterns over and over until they are neural pathways in our brain allows us to get a lot of work done in short order. When we know how to do something, we can move into action and accomplish our goals. We don't need to think about every step.

Consider this example. A mid-size nonprofit has a board nomination meeting this week. Their lone researcher is asked for a list of donor names for board nominations by the next day. The request is the same as the past five years, so she is well practiced. She pulls the top 50 donors from the database. She pulls out last year's board nomination Excel spreadsheet and populates it with this year's top 50 names, keeping the same notes on any names that are still in this group. She inputs the wealth rating for each. She adds in total giving and the last two gifts from each donor. She notes key relationships in the organization. She also adds in volunteer activity and leadership roles for the past five years. She then sorts the list based on how many of the donors have all these categories filled. She does a further sort by the last two gifts given, prioritizing those that were six figures or higher. Finally, she sorts based on wealth ratings. Her final list has 10 names, and she emails the list to her colleague. She has spent two hours on the project. The request was filled efficiently, without her needing to think through each part of the project.

When asked the next morning why there are no women on the list, she notes that while there were women in the original pool, they did not rise to the top 10. The list moves forward, with a note that there were no women on it this year. The standard request received the standard response, all in a timely fashion.

Neither the colleague nor the researcher paused to consider the inputs:

- The colleague didn't specifically ask for women on the list.
- The researcher did not know that wealth ratings are normally higher for men than women, underrepresenting their potential (more on this in the Design section).
- Even if she did know that fact, she had not yet developed a new research process to search women's capacity with alternative tools.

This is not about one person doing anything wrong. It is about facing the reality that these learned practices are seared into us. And we should be grateful! Consider all the choices involved in fundraising for each donor we work with:

- How we identify and qualify the prospects.
- How we cultivate and engage them.
- How we design and make asks for support.
- How we steward the donors.

And there are so many parts of fundraising not even included in the above bullets! Fundraising processes are incredibly complex with thousands of actions involved. Multiply the number of actions by all the humans you interact with to raise funds, internally and externally. We could not possibly meet our annual goals if we had to think through each of those choices every time. So, we have templates for how we research, how we qualify, how we do a cultivation event, how we ask and how we track gifts and acknowledge donors. When anyone is asked to deliver on a project, the first step is often to check in with colleagues to find out if there are any past templates or guidelines to use.

When we open our eyes to our best-practice story and the thousands of practices that have been created from it, we can begin to imagine alternative ways of handling the simple request to create a board nomination list to meet the new goal of including women.

Doing things differently might have led to more women on the submitted list:

- Different leadership commitment to diversity among volunteer leaders,
- Different leadership communication (increase gender equity on the board),
- Different request (specific detail on the desire for more women on the list),
- Different awareness (what are alternative ways to track women's wealth?), and
- Different practices (designing a new list that includes the breadth of women's wealth capacity).

Organizational Impact

No one person is at fault. Individual stories and well-honed practices become organizational structures. While many leaders know that it is a bottom-line imperative to pay attention to women, very few universities or nonprofits have specific strategies to increase women's roles as leaders or philanthropists. Among a group of surveyed nonprofits with assets greater than $25 million, 40 percent said their organizations were not attending to women as donors (Di Mento 2014).

Why is that? As my colleague says regularly: "Organizations are perfectly designed to get the results they get." WPI recently reported:

When a group of fundraisers at a conference was asked why organizations would not attend to women as donors, they quickly identified five reasons: (1) organizational leadership is predominately male, (2) events are tailored for men, (3) data systems list males as main prospects, (4) board recruitment is male-focused, and (5) women are dispersed to auxiliary boards or other entities perceived as less important. (Tempel, Seiler and Burlingame 2016)

With organizational structures rooted in the 1950s and 1960s, we unconsciously focus on men, even when we *know* that we should do our work differently. This bias is acknowledged by Matthew Lambert, vice president of institutional advancement at the College of William & Mary who is leading a university-wide initiative there to increase women's leadership and philanthropy.

Like any good development officer, I knew it was always better to engage both partners in a relationship, but more frequently I found myself meeting with men at their downtown offices in Manhattan, Chicago, Washington, and San Francisco because that was easiest for me. What I should have known is that my convenience might be quite detrimental to their long term philanthropic support. The research is clear that it is essential to also include women in these conversations if we want to maximize giving. (Lambert 2016)

As Lambert suggests, "knowing" something is not the same as taking new actions. Without the transformation that comes with committing to and practicing new behaviors, no change occurs.

Lambert was not the only person responsible for the exclusion of women from his visits. The researcher likely was not asked to provide background on the women who were in the households visited. There were no past notes from previous visits on how decisions were made in that household because no one ever asked. The major-gift fundraiser was not having his performance measured on the number of women visited in his portfolio, so he was not pushing for women to be included. The writer of the briefing didn't pause and realize that the scheduled meeting did not include the wife or female partner. No one sent up a red flag, and so the trip unfolded as so many do.

When we are asked to do something, all parts of the system automatically try to fit that request into known practices. Why? Because that is most efficient. The system doesn't stop to ponder; all individuals who are part of a request move forward automatically. If change is desired, *many* parts of the organization must be part of interrupting the autopilot response. No one person makes change happen, no matter how committed or passionate.

Myths Also Get in Our Way

I recently asked a leader of advancement at a state college if she used different approaches in working with women versus men donors on her campus. This was not meant to be a trick question. I was very curious, as she had been a leader in sorority fundraising and had demonstrated an understanding of how women give. Without missing a beat, she said: "Women are much harder. Give me a male donor any day."

I hear this story over and over—women are harder to work with. A story repeated over and over can become a myth that most people believe. A myth may have a kernel of truth, but it's not necessarily accurate. Let's consider the facts and reframe the story.

As noted in Chapter 1, we know that women consider a myriad of facts and dimensions when making consumer or family decisions. Women ask more questions and look at more details before getting to "yes" or "no." They want their gifts to have an impact. Just as women are more discerning in making financial investments and asking more questions, so, too, they assess their philanthropic decisions. A reframed view of this behavior might be "women are discerning" instead of "women are harder." This level of inquiry and fact-checking by women has not stopped our country's financial money managers from focusing on women. They know that is where the wealth is and will continue to be.

I am empathetic to the leader I spoke with, because I know she is responsible for meeting a very large fundraising goal. Fundraisers are under major pressure. They have limited time and often choose to visit with the donors who can help immediately. When we are under pressure, it is normal to revert to what we've done successfully before. When a woman doesn't respond as anticipated and, in fact, asks more questions, gives less than asked or doesn't agree to be on a board, we turn and focus on those who do respond in *the way we prefer.* A consequence of moving on is that we suboptimize what this woman might give us when she is satisfied with her due diligence.

In addition, we might share what happened with our colleagues. These stories build and collectively we begin to internalize the myth: "It is harder to raise money from women." I question the myth that women are harder. I believe they are just *different.* It is the mismatched application of our well-honed approaches to women that makes it seem harder, because we are setting ourselves up for one preferred result, mainly a quick answer and preferably a gift, but we get another. If we adjust our expectations, "hard" becomes "THIS is the approach" for women.

Beth Mann is the vice president for institutional advancement at the Jewish Federations of North America (JFNA). Women's philanthropy has long been a strong core of JFNA and the 148 Jewish federations around North America, starting in the 1970s with the creation of the Lions of Judah (LOJ). LOJ has a minimum, unrestricted annual gift of $5,000 and nine other giving levels up to $250,000-plus. There are 17,500 Lions of Judah who, along with those women who give solely through the local federations' women's philanthropy departments, gave $200 million last year, with an average gift of more than $10,000. It is important to note that this does not include all the other gifts made by the many women who give to their local federation through vehicles other than women's philanthropy, such as those who give a family gift together with their spouses.

Mann insists that although engaging women in the work of the community can be labor-intensive, the time spent in answering questions, showing the intended impact and designing women's involvement is well worth the work. She sets the expectation to have at least two meetings to get to know a woman's interests and motivations, without mentioning an ask. With that adjustment, Mann finds that women who support their federation are more deeply engaged, often taking on volunteer roles that lighten the load, such as organizing, training, calling and building relationships with other prospects. In addition, they include their families and personal networks so there is also a beneficial leverage effect. The annual financial results speak for themselves.

There are other myths that we might hold and unconsciously pass on to our colleagues:

- Women are less philanthropic than men.
- Women defer to their spouses in charitable decision-making.
- Women do not make big gifts.

The research in Chapter 1 debunks these myths. If you check in with yourself and across your team, you may find you have other assessments, or stories, about working with women and asking for their support. Our challenge is to face myths directly and consider where they came from and how they may be unconsciously influencing our actions.

Using curiosity and commitment as our tools, we can consciously become aware of and address something that is, by nature, unconscious and deep in our neural pathways. When we are not aware, we can miss information and opportunities. Awareness opens up space to observe our responses and consider new choices, rather than just react.

Only when we grow our awareness can we truly translate the clear research about how women give into specific "best practices" designed for women.

Chapter 4

LESSONS LEARNED

"Too often [university] leadership perceives women's philanthropy as the caboose rather than an engine capable of carrying a heavy load."
—Debra Mesch and Andrea Pactor, *Women's Philanthropy on Campus*

Research, awareness, and qualitative data help open the door to new goals and actions. Before designing your unique organizational initiative, let's review programs that intentionally focused on women's philanthropy over the past 25 years. These lessons learned may also help you discern how to move forward.

In 2009, WPI published a paper on "Women's Philanthropy on Campus." At that time, they found that there were more than 3,000 co-ed colleges and universities in our country, but fewer than 10 percent had focused fundraising intentionally on women in the previous 20 years (Mesch and Pactor 2009). Today, we have a few more co-ed colleges and universities, and a few more women's initiatives have started. However, because some programs folded, we still hover at the 10 percent benchmark. There are even fewer intentional programs in the nonprofit sector. Not counting women's foundations and community giving circles, the most prominent nonprofits that intentionally engage philanthropic women can be counted on one hand: American Red Cross's Tiffany Circle, the Jewish Federations' Lions of Judah and the United Way of America's Women United.

Many colleagues and I have tracked these various initiatives and programs focused on women. My 22 years of review have led me to see common practices and note two key lessons from which we can all learn.

Common Practices

Many universities have thoughtfully designed women's "programs" or "initiatives" that blend women's preference to connect and collaborate with the desire for engagement before philanthropic asks. Common elements across these programs include the following.

- *Membership.* This is far and away the most popular design, given women's preferences to netweave and work together. The organization forms a group, council or circle of 100-plus women. This group meets annually or biennially, enabling women to connect with each other and the organization. Many, although not all, programs require their members to make annual gifts of specific amounts, most often ranging from $1,000 to $10,000. Other programs require an annual gift without a specific amount. Many follow a giving-circle model, in which members provide their annual gifts and then collectively allocate those funds for programs that benefit the organization. The membership approach may involve a pipeline of associate councils or groups for younger women or female students. Through service on committees, time to netweave during events and opportunities to hear from inspirational speakers, the membership model creates an important community for those involved.
  - A variation of the membership approach is the creation of a smaller community of women with higher capacity to give significant gifts. The minimum giving threshold might be $25,000 or higher. This is an "elite" council or group; it often has a reputation of cachet and influence in the organization.
- *Gateway event.* This offers women a way to connect with the institution through a stimulating event that includes opportunities to hear from organizational, faculty or program leaders and attend programs rich in content. The event is the catalyzing gateway to start or rekindle a connection. Once connected, the women self-select future methods of staying engaged, from simply reading regular newsletters to going to other events or volunteering. After "finding" these women, the institution can begin cultivation.

- *Connection between women supporters and leaders and beneficiaries of the organization.* These are not formal mentoring programs, but stimulating gatherings that bring women back to campus, headquarters or other regional settings to connect with those who are benefitting from the work. Women on both sides of this relationship feel enriched by the experience, while the organization deepens its relationship with the donors in a unique manner. Examples are connecting alumnae to current students on campus or connecting women philanthropists in a community to those they are supporting in a job-training program.
- *Leadership.* A handful of programs focus on building the number of women in the leadership pipeline and placing women in volunteer leadership positions. While traditionally this might be an internal organizational process, some programs intentionally engage women donors and volunteers to help create awareness about the current proportion of women leaders as volunteers at an organization, participate in setting benchmark goals for the future, and help build relationships with women to widen the pool of future leaders.

Some initiatives combine these models. A membership program might also have a big annual event at the headquarters to engage established members and newly identified women, during which there might be a connecting event with the organization's women leaders. There are many ways to engage women and while the above were the most common, there are successful programs with other approaches. What works are programs designed specifically to connect with what resonates for *your* women stakeholders, tied to your organizational priorities and tailored to your unique organizational culture.

Key Lessons

As you design your approach, it may help to bear in mind two key lessons I learned from programs created prior to 2013:

1. Women often were treated as a separate niche group, which limited the sustainability of such programs; and
2. Women's programs designed primarily for engagement did not always see significant growth in philanthropy.

The Niche Program

The early programs were often created as silo initiatives for women, designed with one to three specific ways to engage them and staffed with a mid-level career person. For instance, I ran the President's Council of Cornell Women in the mid-1990s, just a few years after it was created. I was five years into my university fundraising career and was the sole staff person for a council with more than 700 successful and engaged alumnae. PCCW was not linked to the rest of the development functions at that time. Rarely was I asked for my input about large gift strategies for these donors. Rarely did other fundraisers join in any events we developed for our members to meet the women and further their relationships. I heard similar stories of non-integration from other colleagues running women's programs at the time.

Many programs that began in the late 1980s to early 2000s started in a similar fashion. They were "niches" for women who had capacity to give but had not been cultivated to be brought together in stimulating, engaging and connecting ways. This connection to each other and the organization invariably opened excitement and enthusiasm. It was a relief and felt supportive to connect with other women leaders who cared about the mission and faced similar struggles in their professional lives.

However, in creating a "niche" program, we also built an artificial framework that holds the organization back from growing women's support sustainably and significantly. I use the word "artificial" because, as Lisa Witter and Lisa Chen write in their book, *She Spot*: "Women are not a niche. They are *the* audience." It's time to "ditch the niche" (Witter and Chen 2008, 6, 5).

WPI's *Women's Philanthropy on Campus* report (Mesch and Pactor 2009, 20) reviewed more than two dozen early programs and wrote about why some of these programs failed:

- A mid-level manager (most often a woman) creates the initiative, and the institution marginalizes it.
- When the mid-level manager leaves, the institutional memory about the program leaves with her.
- The institution fails to invest the long-term human and financial capital needed to build the program.
- The program is maintained in isolation and not integrated into the total development strategy.
- Development staff see the women's philanthropy initiative as competition to ongoing efforts, such as the annual fund or alumni giving.

- When there is no return on investment in the first year of the program's operation, the institution terminates the program.
- Some development staff are resistant to change and reluctant to change the status quo.

My own addition after reviewing many initiatives is that there were few metrics to measure success. No one measured the return on investment systematically. Given that the programs were "extras" and not core to the development functions, few organizations created benchmarks and consistently tracked and reported related changes in gifts, donors, participation and leadership.

These separate initiatives for women did create value in many ways. They successfully connected women to the organization, its beneficiaries and to peers. They also expanded women's understanding of the life of the nonprofit or university and important issues it faced. These programs also contributed greatly to our understanding of what works and what doesn't work, as we developed fundraising practices to better fit women.

So, now we know it's time to "ditch the niche" and integrate women into all parts of our fundraising. Plus, times have changed. I have found in many recent focus groups and surveys that many women do not want to be separated in philanthropy efforts. While they often enjoy connecting and collaborating with each other, they also desire to be part of a larger solution that will require all voices at the table.

Knowing that women are the main audience and when you focus on women, you get the men and their families, then the entire model can move toward a more integrated set of activities and behaviors. You may design a programmatic means to connect women to each other while growing their engagement, leadership and philanthropy. In addition, consider how you'll leverage your design with your fundraising colleagues across the organization in commitment, collaboration, behaviors and support to grow women's philanthropy. In the chapter of this book that focuses on destiny, you'll see how UCLA transformed an early membership program into an inclusive initiative that is more integrated today across campus.

The Engagement/Philanthropy Connection

Early engagement designs for women's programs included the hope that the significant gifts from involved women would begin and grow. That hope did not always materialize. There was a belief, conscious or unconscious, that "if you build it, they will come, *and give.*" A fundraising belief, based on men, is that there is a natural progression from engagement to leadership volunteer roles to significant philanthropy.

Do women have this same progression? They may not. In Chapter 1, we learned that while women now have the influence and capacity to give more and ARE giving more than men in similar situations, women have distinct giving behaviors. While many clearly say that they prefer to be engaged before they are asked for a gift, they also:

- *Focus on high-impact over high-profile roles.* This may mean that women don't consciously seek leadership titles and roles. They may prefer to stay engaged in activities that allow them to see impact on beneficiaries directly.
- *Spread their giving.* This may mean you design overt conversations to answer questions and help women design a path to a significant gift.
- *Prefer to engage collaboratively.* Many women like to solve problems with others, using their time, talent and funding. This may mean that a group of women could achieve significant influence and philanthropy together, to a greater degree than you might have anticipated, perhaps in addition to individual giving.

Listening to many women stakeholders in many interviews, I've learned that women don't necessarily follow the same steps to significant giving as men. So, our work may not be about urging them forward on the current "best practice" path, but rather helping them carve out their own process. Part III of this book, which focuses on the design phase, will provide specific examples of organizations that are forging new ways for women to share *all* the resources they have to offer for missions they care about—time, expertise, intellect, network *and* significant philanthropic support.

DISCOVERY SUMMARY

At this juncture, you and your discovery team have likely learned:

1. Gender matters. Women and men have different patterns of philanthropic behavior.

2. Focusing on women is an economic decision; it will impact your bottom line.

3. Women are philanthropic decision-makers and often give more than men.

4. How much your women donors currently give and how much you are losing each year by not connecting to women.

5. Specific input, desires and possibilities from your women stakeholders.

6. Fundraising best practices which were designed for men may not resonate with women.

7. The need to confront our myths about women's philanthropy because they may be constraining women's gifts.

8. Women today want to connect with each other *and* be integrated with men as well as women to tackle issues.

9. Adaptation of fundraising behaviors to include women is needed across the organization. Niche programs are less effective.

10. Women's progression on their philanthropic path can be different than men's.

In addition to these 10 general points, you've gained a wealth of information specific to your organization. This information likely was never gathered before and will be key building blocks for your next steps. This discovery data is your guide and your foundation. You will regularly refer back to what you learned to create your unique initiative to intentionally invite in women who care about your critical mission.

Part II

DREAM

Chapter 5

IMAGINE

"We do not need magic to transform our world. We carry all the power we need inside ourselves already. We have the power to imagine better."
—J.K. Rowling, Harvard Commencement Speech

During the discovery process, you likely gained far more than simple knowledge. You started with a structured system shaped by historic practices, founded in how men give. Your engagement in inquiry and discovery opened minds and created some permeability in your thinking and that of your peers about the design of the organization. When something is permeable, more can pass through—information, support, ideas, sustenance, light. This permeability came from your curiosity and openness to alternatives. You have met around tables or on conference calls with your team where you posed questions about the research, your data, your past experiences, the voices of your women donors and what you heard about other programs. You delved into stories and discussed trends and values. You may have even extended this curiosity and awareness to others in your organization.

You already may be instinctively leaning toward potential new behaviors. Humans move into action; this instinct has always kept us safe and helped us survive. But I want your organization to thrive, not just survive. So, in this space between everything you've learned and your response to that newfound knowledge, I want you to pause. Reflect, review and evaluate your discovery data before you try to discern how you will proceed. This important process will open thinking and generate more ideas. There will be key themes in your review that may become elements in your vision and practices in your design.

From your own data, donor stories and reflections on your development practices, what are your top takeaways? What did you hear, read and feel that might be relevant? What did you learn about your cultural strengths and values? What was revealed in the philanthropic stories of your women donors? What themes were present in your survey or focus groups? What did you glean from how your donors are currently giving? Where are the gaps? The missed opportunities? What was the top message that was repeated over and over? Do you have new questions? If so, some of these questions might even move you to look at the data again or follow up with your donors and stakeholders.

Finally, review the staff interviews and consider the reality of where your organization is today. What opportunities are mentioned the most? Where do you still need to make key progress? Are you gearing up for a campaign and need a broader pool of donors? Is there a commitment to diversify your funding streams? Is there a desire to increase diversity on boards and committees?

The answers to these questions are potential design components for your actions. When you build a house, you have a wide range of materials to choose from. You might walk into Home Depot and feel overwhelmed by all the options. But gradually you start feeling energy as you are drawn to some items over others. In this moment of pause, you should rumble with all the inputs you've received and see which ideas rise to the top for you and your discovery team.

Whether you create a written report about your discovery process, or take a less formal approach to organizing your ideas (I like to group categories of themes written on big sticky notes on a whiteboard), you will find it helpful to have the salient facts at your fingertips to create your vision and then your design.

You are now ready to move into the "dream" stage, a simple yet profound leadership exercise to create a compelling mental picture of what is possible. Those imagined possibilities will become your practical vision, the architectural plan that guides your choices. Once you have a clear mental picture, you have already started the change process.

The Power of a Declared Vision

Integrating women across your fundraising processes is not an all or nothing act. You could just start from where you are today. However, starting without a vision can be ineffective. My favorite quote from *Alice in Wonderland* illustrates this point:

> "Would you tell me, please, which way I ought to go from here?," asked Alice.
> "That depends a good deal on where you want to get to," said the Cat.
> "I don't much care where—" said Alice.
> "Then it doesn't matter which way you go," said the Cat.
> "—so long as I get SOMEWHERE," Alice added as an explanation.
> "Oh, you're sure to do that," said the Cat, "if you only walk long enough."

In other words, without defining your desired outcomes, you can work on something, but you can't get "there," because you have not picked a clear destination. Without a goal or direction, how can you design the specific actions to get "there," and how do you know that the actions you do choose will be successful?

Declaring a clear vision is a powerful organizing tool for individuals, teams and organizations. I learned this from the Strozzi Institute, the original architect of "embodied leadership." They train individuals in a unique approach that combines the latest in neuroscience, holistic practice, action-oriented communication and mindfulness.

The institute notes the importance of making declarations:

> We create the future through language. When we make a declaration, we make a commitment to a future space of possibility. Until we distinguish this future possibility in language, there is no such future to move toward, there are no actions to take to fulfill on the declaration, and others cannot help us fulfill our declared goals. Of course, life unfolds and moves forward, regardless of whether we speak a vision of the future or not. But if we are in the game of choosing and creating a life, the declaration sets a direction and galvanizes our intention, much like a compass bearing sets a course and guides us to a specific destination. The skill of making a declaration is a fundamental skill of leadership, whether in leading our own lives or in leading others. (Strozzi Institute 2016)

Creating an inspiring vision of the future is powerful and brings about change. For instance:

- In 1961, President John F. Kennedy declared that the U.S. should set a goal of "landing a man on the moon and returning him safely to earth." This was unimaginable at the time, and yet achieving that vision by 1969 advanced our country and the world in science, technology and engineering.
- In 1980, Bill Gates made the Microsoft mission statement public: "We will put a computer on every desk and in every home." This was audacious for its time. Today, we live in homes filled with computers of all sizes, including those in our hands.
- In 2007, sisters Swanee Hunt and Helen LaKelly Hunt declared that in three years 150 women would commit to a gift of $1 million or more to support women and girls. They had no prospect list—it was simply a bold goal. They achieved that goal in less than three years, and the global nonprofit Women Moving Millions was born.

These lofty examples might make you shrink back and say, "We just want to raise more money." Of course, that is a goal, but why? Imagining in detail a hoped-for future can be compelling—not just for one person, but for many. Even creating and articulating the imagined future begins to move us forward and draw others to our vision. To imagine begins the change. It is the seed of transformation.

But change is hard, so we must have a persuasive reason to go through it, something to pull us forward into new behaviors, conversations, actions and processes. Think of your own life. When you made a significant change, what sense of purpose drove you? A friend of mine declared she would own a home at a time when that felt financially impossible to her. She tore out pictures of homes she wanted, she circled neighborhoods on maps, she shared this goal with her friends and colleagues. That declaration organized her behavior, and she began to make choices that aligned with her goal and said no to choices that did not. She started working with a financial advisor for the first time, changed what she was charging as a consultant, chose new spending and saving habits, enlisted the help of experts to learn about mortgages and credit for first-time homeowners. She bought her first home within two years. Achieving this declared vision forever changed my friend. She has become that declaration—a homeowner with financial habits that keep her in her home.

Teams can make bold declarations and transform themselves as well. Hurricane Katrina hit in 2005, when I was leading the fundraising at the American

Red Cross. The Red Cross received $2 billion in donations in just four months, a volume we had never before experienced. Our acknowledgment team became backlogged immediately on thank-you letters to donors, sending them out two months late. After analyzing the situation, the team declared that accurate, personalized letters of thanks would go out two weeks after a gift arrived. This was an audacious commitment when the backlog was still growing hourly. Yet, they transformed the processes and achieved the goal within 12 weeks. That commitment drove the creation of new systems and partnerships. The bank lock-box reports, the data downloads, the requests and expectations of frontline fundraisers and the review and signature processes all changed. Not only did the team meet its goal for Katrina donors, but it began operating differently across all fundraising efforts for future acknowledgments.

Compelling visions can create sustainable change in an organization. We discussed the lessons learned from early women's philanthropy programs in Chapter 4. Those designed as niche projects and isolated from the rest of the development and alumni teams had neither a vision that aligned across the organization's leadership nor engaged colleagues from all parts of the institution willing to make the changes necessary for success. For this reason, many early programs either did not survive, remained marginalized or needed later reinvention by a visionary leader.

Here are two powerful visions for women's philanthropy that spurred transformation in their respective universities:

In 2015, Duke University declared that it would create a fundraising and leadership culture more attuned to the full strength of the alumni body. To achieve this declaration, they started with an intentional focus on women and created this vision:

> The Women in Leadership and Philanthropy Initiative aims to more fully integrate alumnae into volunteer and philanthropic leadership ranks at Duke in order to better support the university's trajectory. We will advance alumnae into key volunteer leadership roles at Duke, and maximize alumnae giving to the Duke Forward Campaign and beyond. Moreover, we will broaden the development culture at Duke to better identify, cultivate, solicit, and steward women donors.

With this vision, Duke University capitalized on existing strengths and programs and imagined new models of activity and inclusion. The WiLP initiative was the genesis of the Duke Women's Impact Network, also called WIN. Members of WIN have given $100K in cumulative lifetime giving. These members stay engaged through deep and influential support of their alma mater. They cultivate and partner with younger alumnae and champion volunteer leadership that is more representative of its alumni and student body.

In 2016, the leadership of the College of William & Mary's advancement team declared:

> William & Mary honors the power of women. They are involved in every facet of the university's success. We recognize their central role in engagement and philanthropy. Women will represent 50 percent of volunteer leaders and private giving by 2020. By increasing their active participation in all aspects of university life, William & Mary will create a culture that empowers women and enhances their impact on campus and community. The Alma Mater of the Nation will serve as a global model for others who strive to produce and celebrate women leaders.

This vision includes several significant commitments that have already mobilized changes in how the members of William & Mary's advancement team work together and with other groups across campus. One example is the pledge to have women fill 50 percent of volunteer leadership positions by 2020. In 2015, women made up 37 percent of all volunteer board members. As of June 2017, following just 18 months of intentional focus, the boards were 59 percent men and 41 percent women. William & Mary is well along the path toward achieving the 50 percent goal. To do so, they have put in place new accountabilities—a partnership with research staff to create pipelines that both meet board criteria and include women, a system to track prospects' retirements well in advance, on-going conversations with board liaisons and constant monitoring and nudging of prospects.

These two transformative visions have several key components in common:

- *Collective vision.* Part of any strategic plan is the creation of a vision. Traditional strategic planning processes often have the leaders create this vision and cascade it down through the organization. The creation of the two vision statements above brought many voices into the process to participate in and influence the agreements made to pursue specific outcomes. This participation also increased the likelihood that those involved would commit to the goals and objectives they helped create. This level of participation also can accelerate the movement from vision to action. Your interviews and data collection in the inquiry stage will help to build this collective voice, input and commitment from many.

- *Leadership engagement.* Leaders, both staff and volunteer, were part of the collective vision, not absent or set apart. Their commitment to the new possibilities outlined in the vision, and their willingness to be held accountable for tracking and reporting results, was crucial to the universities' ability to follow through and make sustained progress. In addition, the staff leaders were empowered to make decisions and/or had the ear and support of decision makers.

- *Discovery-Driven.* Both visions were tied to the data and women's stories collected in the discovery phase, as well as their organization's strengths, values and situations at the time they were created. Duke was already committed to the Duke Forward Campaign, which offered an opportunity to create the WiLP initiative. William & Mary had a new vice president committed to diversity, its own campaign launch and an upcoming 100th anniversary celebrating women being admitted to the college.

- *Measurable Outcomes.* The compelling visions stated intended results. They were not vapid and high level. They included specific details about the desired future.

- *Integration.* Change can never happen in a vacuum, or with one person. Both visions included integration of actions across the development culture and beyond. Sustainable growth of women's support will only come when many in the organization commit to the vision, own their roles and report on their progress.

   To maximize integration across a development department and beyond, teams in the department can build their own vision statements to fulfill organizational goals. When an overarching organizational vision is created, unique team visions are needed to focus and organize each group that contributes to the success of the whole. Everyone has a role. Below are some examples from William & Mary's various advancement teams. Each of them ties into the overall vision.

   - *Advancement Services:* Our team uses data-driven analytics to identify female prospects by using models to explore what inspires women to give and engage. Research takes a women-focused approach by placing an equal emphasis on single women and both members of a couple when creating research briefings. Prospect management is intentional about ensuring a 50 percent balance of women in portfolios. This allows William & Mary to meet or exceed donor expectations and better acknowledge the contributions of our female donors.

- *Frontline Fundraisers:* The frontline team creates a powerful community of alumnae by teaching, renewing, inspiring, building and empowering women. We advance women's philanthropy at William & Mary by creating and executing strategies that actively identify, engage and celebrate women. By establishing a culture of inclusive and values-driven outreach, women will increase philanthropy and involvement at a leadership level, resulting in 50 percent of private giving and holding 50 percent of the volunteer leadership roles by 2020.

- *Advancement Communications:* William & Mary sets the standard in communicating compelling and inspiring stories about the remarkable impact women make in their communities, the nation and the world. We actively pursue female voices and stories in the areas where they are most passionate. In an effort to increase engagement with their alma mater we have committed to providing equal treatment of genders across all communication channels. We continually assess success through surveys and focus groups.

- *Alumnae Engagement:* The alumnae team is committed to optimizing meaningful lifelong engagement with women that starts at day one of their William & Mary experience. We connect students to alumnae, alumnae to each other and alumnae to their alma mater through intellectual, professional and cultural opportunities that celebrate achievements and inspire increased engagement and philanthropy.

Create Your Own Compelling Vison

Gather Your Team

As with your discovery work, creating your vision is not to be undertaken by a lone individual. Form a team and meet to introduce and discuss your vision. Answer these questions: Who should be involved? What relevant voices do we want at the table? Your answers will be unique to your organization. The key is to draw on a range of perspectives. It is also helpful to look for diverse styles—bring on board some people who are visual and might draw images and others who are primarily verbal. One organization included in this book gathered the leaders of the development team, while three others included volunteers from their discovery team as well as development staff. The diversity of your group will accelerate commitment to the vision and ownership of the achievements.

Review Discovery Material

1. Review the categories you've gathered from your discovery.
   a. What did you see in your quantitative data? Where might there be an opportunity for growth? You might see it in annual fundraising, while others might focus on major or principal gifts.
   b. Review the qualitative input you received from women stakeholders and consider the high points, wishes and themes. What are they longing for? What more are they willing to do with you and for you? What did they say it will take to catalyze their increased support? What do they desire in terms of impact and personal contribution?
   c. Also review the feelings that emerged during your discovery. When did you feel pride? When did you feel excited by a possibility, or a sense of purpose? When did you have an "aha" moment and what energy did it unleash? These are not simply feel-good questions. A compelling vision will include affect words that stir up images of a better world. Reflect on the declaration made by William & Mary. They "honor the power of women" and will be a "global leader for others."
2. Keep in mind your organization's key values and strengths. What makes your organization what it is today? It's always easiest to build from the core strengths of your organization rather than start from scratch.
3. Consider the organizational effect of a powerful vision. That is, how would it feel to be part of this team achieving this audacious goal? Given our passion for fundraising and working with donors, why not also envision extraordinary teamwork?
4. Consider where you are in your fundraising maturity. A compelling vision stretches the status quo, but it won't be inspiring or successful if it feels too far away. Are you early in building your fundraising strategies, or do you have a robust team and protocols raising consistent

dollars? Are you thinking about or entering a campaign? Are you concerned about shifting the culture and want more women to be involved in decision-making? Stretch out from your current stage toward your vision. You can intentionally focus on women one step at a time based on where you are today and what you long for next.

Dream Exercise

With your review top of mind, spend time in small groups discussing this scenario:

Imagine you left your organization this year to pursue other interests. Five years later, you return and are told that your organization is successful beyond your hopes with women's philanthropy. It's generating great results and the donors and all the stakeholders who worked on it are so proud of the roles they played.

1. Describe what you witness in written bullets to be shared.
2. What was the primary achievement that occurred, and what did it look like?
3. What is significantly different now, thanks to your organization's work?
4. Who were the key stakeholders and donors?
5. What are people proud of?
6. How was the vision realized? You left knowing great change was in order!
7. What were critical moments or turning points?

Now discuss these questions and create a draft vision based on your answers.

Come together with the other small groups to share your visions. The exercise is most successful when feedback focuses on what you appreciate about each group's ideas, avoiding criticism. Make suggestions about what might be added to each idea to make it more complete.

From this group discussion, you likely will see common themes and opportunities. As with any process, at this point you can sift through and choose the themes that energize the most, offer the greatest opportunities for improvement and pose new possibilities that build on your core strengths.

Your compelling vision will start emerging from your discussion across the groups. You will begin to see many of the following elements:

- Stretch the status quo.
- Challenge common assumptions or routines.

- Help suggest real possibilities that represent a desired image for the organization and its stakeholders.
- Achieve outstanding results, far greater than today, producing these results in a practical, effective manner.
- Make an extraordinary team possible so that you experience not just great results but also personal transformation.

Circle phrases that are compelling. Using a multi-voting process, ask individuals to rank those phrases. From this point, draft a single vision. It won't yet be "pretty" but it will contain the essential images and aspirations that will keep the organization galvanized in action. Later, someone can take the draft and tighten it for final review and affirmation.

This process does not take long with intentional facilitation. It can be designed for completion in a half-day, across several mornings or one part of a two-day retreat. It does require having the right stakeholders in the room, as well as the input from many other stakeholders gathered in the inquiry.

It also takes willingness to be creative and imaginative in considering the future. We often don't give ourselves time to do this. We move fast, make quick decisions to execute tasks and use our left brain to consider logic. This process engages our right brain in imagery and creativity. It also calls upon our intuition. We often don't take time to listen to our intuition. But when we do, we find it is full of ideas and connections.

The result of the few hours spent on this exercise will be your unique vision for how *you* will deepen your connection with women and grow philanthropy. It will be focused, measurable and, most of all, compelling across your organization. Unlike Alice in Wonderland, you will know where you want to go and will now be able to design specific, efficient and integrated actions to achieve your results.

Chapter 6

INTENTIONS

"All great acts are ruled by intention. What you mean is what you get."
—Brenna Yovanoff, *The Replacement*

With a vision in mind, we now want more clarity. Visions can be inspiring. Yet we need to ground them with a few key intentions, or areas of focus, before acting. What guiding strategies will serve as the pillars supporting our new vision? What organizational framework will help us move forward? What other actions are needed to begin?

Take again the example of Duke University. Its vision: "The Women in Leadership and Philanthropy Initiative (WiLP) aims to more fully integrate alumnae into volunteer and philanthropic leadership ranks at Duke in order to better support the university's trajectory."

The university chose four areas of focus for its work.

- Alumnae engagement: Targeted those with the capacity to contribute significant volunteer leadership and philanthropic support.
- Women in leadership: Created new ways to encourage alumnae to participate and volunteer for leadership roles at Duke.
- Institutional culture: Recalibrated Duke's fundraising practices to include the motivations, concerns, and needs of its alumnae.
- Resources and infrastructure: Designed the staff, volunteer, technical and administrative support necessary to achieve the objectives.

These intentions were very much connected to where Duke was at that point in its fundraising. To more fully integrate alumnae, the university could have said "engage all alumnae" or decided to showcase the women who were already in leadership positions, rather than focusing on alumnae with capacity. Duke's intentions were tied directly to that moment in time, its strengths, and what its leadership heard their stakeholders say. The university had just launched the $3.25 billion "Duke Forward Campaign" and wanted to grow the number of women visibly giving significant gifts to the effort, so the development team chose to target their engagement efforts to achieve that goal. In addition, they understood clearly that women step into leadership differently than men. They wanted to honor that reality and create new ways to ask women to participate as leaders.

In another example, the University of San Francisco had the following vision:

> The Women in Philanthropy at USF initiative aims to reconnect alumnae with each other and with the university, provide meaningful engagement opportunities and advance women into volunteer leadership roles. Moreover, it intends to broaden the development culture at USF to better identify, cultivate, solicit, and steward women donors. Together these efforts will build a strong foundation for growing alumnae giving to the university, the campaign, and beyond.

USF's intention to move this vision forward was to first focus on engagement. Different from Duke, the development team in this example wanted to create a gateway for alumnae to re-connect with the school. The university knew that it had let engagement lapse in previous years and wanted to focus on the ways women preferred to connect, both to each other and the university. So, it chose two intentions:

- Meaningful Engagement: Designed significant and impactful ways that women could volunteer and become involved with USF.
- Women in Leadership: Began a systematic review of current boards, councils and committees. This benchmark was designed to help them identify, recruit and groom women for various volunteer roles at USF.

In this example, meaningful engagement was the primary focus for action, and the review of current women's leadership served to gather more discovery data.

Choose Your Intentions

Designing the right intentions to support a vision need not take much time. You will often find them through a review of the discovery data you gathered. The above two examples became apparent during discussion of the information each group compiled on its strengths, needs at that moment and stakeholders' information and interests. They listened to the stories they heard and the opportunities they unearthed. They considered the current, ongoing strategies (such as a campaign, or rebooting alumni engagement). They stayed true to core organizational values, as well as the values expressed by their stakeholders. And they chose a few key levers that would accelerate the achievement of their vision.

As you think about the general research about women's philanthropy, there are three principles you might consider, alone or in combination, as you review your own inquiry data and vision to select intentions: Engagement, Leadership and Philanthropy. Below is a chart to help you visualize them side by side.

This chart does not mean that you need to start with engagement first. I show all three so you can choose the intention that best fits your vision. You may choose all three, or just one to focus on as you begin, as USF did.

In the chart, I've also noted integrative strategy for each design principle. Compelling visions and the resulting designs will acknowledge all the ways that women can provide support for an organization, and recognize the interdependencies between them. We will not accelerate women's philanthropy

	Engagement	Leadership	Philanthropy
Objective	Engage women, based on specific criteria, exposing them to the organization and opportunities to become involved.	Intentional focus to create awareness, support, and paths for women to become volunteer leaders.	Engage women with identified potential for philanthropic leadership.
Integrative Strategy	Build women's engagement that motivates leadership and philanthropy.	Engage women leaders and support their growth as philanthropic leaders.	Engaged women who are leaders and philanthropists will help shift the culture and impact of the organization.
Audience	Large group of women. May or may not be donors.	Women donors with capacity and experience to serve in a leadership role.	Prioritized women donors with the capacity to give at a specified level.

	Engagement	Leadership	Philanthropy
Characteristics	• Collective cultivation • Netweaving with peers • Opportunities to connect with organizational leaders • Education on the impact and beneficiaries of the organization	• Individualized cultivation toward leadership • Connection to other leaders (women and men) • Education on the impact possible at leadership level	• Meaningful personalized engagement • Education about compelling organizational needs • Time for discerning questions
Fundraising Request	May be asked for an annual commitment. Specific annual requests are often at the $1,000 to $10,000 level.	Asked for a leadership gift per the criteria for serving in the leadership role.	• Individual asked for a significant major gift to help achieve an organizational need. • Individuals may be asked as part of a group effort for goal.

if we do not imagine full integration of women into our mission, which will allow the achievement of greater organizational growth—a result much greater than simply raising more funds.

Women know there are multiple ways they can expand their involvement with an organization—working with peers in a way that leverages their collective force, offering their expertise or time, spending time with the beneficiaries of the mission, participating in leadership roles and giving a philanthropic gift. Their goal is to have an impact, and they know it takes more than a single event, gift or role to do so. In one focus group of Duke University stakeholders, the women reinforced the idea that the emphasis of the new initiative should not be to raise more money for Duke, but to *transform Duke*. They wanted to *make a great Duke even better*.

One woman stakeholder at USF said, "This is not about women connecting to each other—a 'tea gathering.' Women are able to change the world. USF has a powerful platform for social justice and women can help bring that out across the country."

I am not recommending a complete overhaul of fundraising operations. You must make informed implementation choices. You can intentionally move toward your organizational vision, which includes the integration of women's support, one step at a time. The action step for each organization is to have a compelling image of future possibility and then set clear intentions about where to start and how to sequence the work, based on your larger vision, resources and the unique moment in time.

I recently had a conversation with Tom Herbert, senior vice president for advancement and president of the Miami Foundation at Miami University in Ohio. Herbert is passionate about engaging women in the life of the university. He pays attention to women's philanthropy research and knows the importance of engaging women directly rather than making assumptions. He holds the long view of the changes he wants to bring about on campus with engaged women, equality of leadership and ever-growing significant gifts. He cannot move intentionally with his vision until he finishes building the development team. However, he is methodically beginning to engage key women stakeholders with his first step. The Miami Initiative for Advancing, Mentoring and Investing in Women—M.I.A.M.I. Women—is a university-wide initiative that works with alumni, campus offices, and student groups in its efforts to encourage and support opportunities for women in leadership. This first focus area is on the road to the larger, integrated vision to which Herbert is committed.

Once chosen, it is important that you make your intentions explicit and public. "This is what we are doing, this is how we are going forward for now and this is why." Making your intentions explicit is crucial to moving from a 30,000-foot vision to a specific set of foci. It helps avoid different interpretations. Create clear organizing principles with which all your stakeholders can connect and work. Otherwise, individuals will do what they believe is best to bring the vision forward. Publicizing objectives is important because people's reputations and trustworthiness are on the line. There is a higher likelihood of on-going actions to achieve success when something is stated, recorded and ultimately tracked.

Sheree Meredith, vice president of philanthropic services at the Hamilton Community Foundation in Canada, has made the goals of "Women 4 Change" very public. This initiative was born in 2012 from two important influences. Supported by the foundation, 10 local women came together to discuss how to increase the effectiveness of their philanthropy. They wanted to have impact in the community, not put names on buildings. At the same time, the foundation did a strategic analysis of its long-time donors and found it was time to engage more women in their 40s and 50s. After six months of reviewing research and discussing goals and options, Women 4 Change was created with a vision to improve the lives of women and girls in Hamilton as well as enable the women of Hamilton to become leaders in philanthropy.

These two organizing principles anchored the resulting design for the initiative. Membership has grown from the original 10 to 70 today, with a wide range of ages. Educational and social opportunities are held throughout the year for women members to learn about finances and philanthropy, as well as needs in the community. Members give to a grants fund that provides financial support for community services for women and girls, and outcomes are tracked so the foundation and members keep learning what works, what doesn't and why. In addition, Women 4 Change undertakes research and publishes papers on key topics important to women and publicly shares the information.

Now that you have chosen your clear intentions, you, too, are ready to move into the design phase!

Part III

DESIGN

Chapter 7

OVERVIEW

*"Human-centered design. Meeting people where they are and really
taking their needs and feedback into account. When you let people
participate in the design process, you find that they often have ingenious
ideas about what would really help them. And it's not a onetime thing;
it's an iterative process."*
—Melinda Gates, interview with *Wired* magazine

Before starting the design process, let's reflect on what you have already
accomplished:

- You have stakeholders who are now aware of your organization's potential economic bottom line if you increase attention to women.
- You have created a village of people around you who are now curious, can ask questions, be engaged, provide support and partner to design ways to connect with women differently. Attention and awareness are no small outcome.
- Your now larger group of involved individuals has created a compelling vision—one that people desire and are willing to make changes to achieve.
- You have clarified the specific intentions of your vision to guide your choice of actions.

You can count on the energy of this process to move people. Beginning
with curiosity about the subject at hand—women's philanthropy—you enlivened yourselves and opened possibilities. You began to soften former unconscious rigidities and shift conversations. Your vision is an inspiring image of

what you are committed to as you integrate women's philanthropy into your larger fundraising efforts. One of the principles of Appreciative Inquiry is "positive image, positive action." Your image is like a thousand dominoes, lined up and ready to be nudged into action, moving in alignment toward completion. Neuropsychology suggests that once this image exists, the change has begun. The philanthropy muscles are warmed up and ready to run.

Sustained change follows when there is a shared awareness and an alignment around a vision of moving to a new possibility. If we try to change first without awareness and alignment, we build new behaviors that won't last. With awareness and alignment, you are leaning in the direction of change, lined up to tackle the challenge and ready to build effectively on your unique opportunities and vision to accelerate women's philanthropy, a critical vehicle to further your organization's mission.

It is time to create your unique design for doing so.

This design section has five chapters, each filled with examples. Each example shared comes from a unique organizational vision and commitment and is intended to ignite your imagination. Choose ideas that may fit your vision and organization and adapt them for your use. The examples offered here are not meant to be a "to-do" list. Some of the options I share may not fit the key themes from your discovery, the culture of your institution or your vision. What you design will be unique to your organization.

I've written this section with three organizing principles in mind:

First, the traditional donor cycle: How do we best **identify** the women with whom to connect? How do we communicate in ways that **inspire**? What are successful ways to **involve** women? How might we ask for their **investment**? Finally, how do we share **impact** with them to deepen their connection? In the five chapters that follow, I will connect the lessons we've learned so far to ground the examples shared. This is a reminder to make contextual design choices that reflect the research as well as an organization's unique stakeholders and strengths.

I use the donor cycle since all fundraisers are familiar with it, and it helps to organize the examples. However, know that I use the word "cycle" loosely. As we collectively deepen our engagement with women and share what we learn, we may find that there is another metaphor to describe how we grow women's philanthropy. Just because our definition of this cycle has worked for many years does not mean that it will end up being the most effective template for how we interact with women. Collectively, we may come up with a new model.

Second, implementing your intentional design: How will you go from the example to *your* specific institutionalized actions? Two components will be needed to successfully implement anything you might choose—"what" and "who."

For instance, let's say your overarching vision is:

> We will be a model of having women contribute equally in all parts of our organization. As a visible reflection of this, we will celebrate an equal number of women as men making gifts in our upcoming campaign.

One of your intentional foci may be women who are now annual donors making a stretch gift to the campaign, either on their own or as part of a couple's gift. A key to achieving this intention may be how you research and qualify this pool of donors.

The "what" concerns the mechanisms for change, those things that need to be acted on, created, improved or transformed *to achieve the vision you have imagined.* These can be processes, partnerships, agreements, training or new tools. These become key elements in implementation. For instance, to identify the annual women donors with capacity to stretch their giving, you may consider:

- Training your researchers on women's philanthropy,
- New research methods geared for women of wealth, and
- New reports on the frequency of women's giving.

The "who" are the actors who can help make the change happen. An actor is anyone who has a direct role in the mechanism you've chosen in support of the vision. Continuing with the identification of women who are ready to stretch their support, sample actors are:

- The researcher and/or database analyst.
- The frontline fundraisers who can ask questions when they meet with women.
- Any intake staff with whom women share information (i.e., admissions, program registration, event RSVP).
- The Board, and/or other volunteers, who can review names and connections.

There are many more stakeholders, of course—the organization's administration, the beneficiaries of future philanthropy, etc. Again, connecting to women cannot be done successfully by one person; it must be integrated with others for sustainability. Think of the actors with a direct role as a subset of all stakeholders involved in this initiative.

Third, metrics: What gets measured gets done. Suggested metrics are in each chapter to help you consider how to create benchmarks and then measure and report on progress. We know metrics are often not created during the excitement of design, or they are not consistently tracked and reported. We saw this from lessons learned from the early women's philanthropy programs. One person can't do everything, including reporting on metrics.

This book is about including many people in your vision and execution. Whether you are a small nonprofit or large university, commit to metrics from the very beginning of design. By using a wider lens to connect with stakeholders, you WILL find the right volunteer, staff member and leadership support to help create your metrics.

Sample metrics to achieve the above vision might include:

- Reports and briefings that present information on both members of a household, with the woman first.
- Quarterly review of what percent of the donor pipeline is female.
- Quarterly review of what percent of visits included women.

With these organizing principles, let's begin with "identify."

Chapter 8

IDENTIFY

"They asked my husband, but not me."
—Focus group quote

Overview

During Discovery, we looked at unconscious stories we might have about women's philanthropy. Many of those stories might be exacerbated by the limitations of your database or constituent-management system. For instance, while most systems today have a field for gender, many organizations do not have policies, procedures and processes that are designed to prioritize or enforce the entry of gender information. If the process is not in place, there likely are inaccuracies when totaling women's giving to your organization, which can perpetuate the story that women are not giving as much as men. If there is no process to combine information about the woman in the household on a male record, we may unconsciously think she is less important because she is not listed whenever that record is pulled. If we automatically address only the man in a thank you letter, we may be continuing a perception that a woman did not influence the gift. New designs for the first step in the donor cycle—identification—will lead later to more effective communication and cultivation for women who care about your mission.

If our current "best practices" in fundraising were created primarily for how men give, so it follows that our data management was designed to provide reports to support that approach. With your intention to focus on women, it then follows that you'll need to rumble with your current data processes. What still works, and what might be limiting us? Recalling the research on women's philanthropy, here are just a few considerations:

- Given that women often choose to donate across many organizations:
  - How do you learn about the totality of their giving?
  - Do you prioritize those women who give frequently across time, even if you only see a few gifts to your organization?
  - What searchable fields do you have to record totality and frequency?
- Given that donating time and effort often precedes giving for women:
  - How do you track a woman's volunteer activities with your organization?
  - How do you analyze the trends of her volunteer activity to strategize future giving?
- Given that women are making more of the philanthropic decisions in the household:
  - How do you find out about the decision-making on each gift?
  - What fields do you have to record this separately and then analyze family trends?
  - Do you have a clear protocol for crediting who actually decided on the gift, or is your default simply the name on the check?
- Given that today's women are earning more, investing more and giving more than generations past:
  - Do you keep separate records for women?
  - Are you setting up Google alerts on female donors, separate from their spouses?
  - Do you record separately the unique assets and income from the woman in a two-person household?
  - Conversely, for a family record, can you aggregate or disaggregate the spouses and children for separate analyses?
- Given that women are becoming more visible and powerful in our society in every way:
  - Do you have a way to measure a woman prospect's influence and impact in her community or sector?
  - Do you have a way to track her leadership roles in her career and community?

The potential adaptions to our data management protocols are thought-provoking. Here is another thought to consider: when we recognize that our data management may be entwined with our unconscious biases, we must also *approach* our research differently. My colleague Haider Ali, formerly the associate director for business intelligence in the McGill University advancement office, said:

> In the traditional model, research has been done like fishing—we ask for information from our data analyst and see what comes up. With women's philanthropy, we are trying to break through inherent biases. I found that flipping my mindset worked better. Flipping meant I looked at trends that were emerging in the real world and analyzed whether those manifested in our giving data. With the traditional mindset, I was asked for giving data, and indeed women were giving less that men in the general population. With a flipped approach, I saw that different generations were behaving differently in the workplace. So, I analyzed the generational giving data and found that the giving growth rate* of young alumnae was outpacing our young alumni. And it is easier to accelerate what is already happening than to grow from scratch. (*Note: this is the rate at which their giving amounts increase.)

Ali's approach is a refreshing, successful model. Start with today's demographic trends. Figure out how to adapt your strategies, tactics and systems (in that order) with the trend in mind.

Design

Face reality with curiosity. Adapt current processes. Create new approaches for research. All of these actions are needed to identify, research, prioritize and report on the women who are giving or might give to you.

Below are many examples of individuals or teams that have found ways to identify and learn more about women. As you read to learn "what" they did (the actions or mechanisms), also pay attention to "who" the key actors were. For some, it helped that leaders were directly involved. In other cases, a group of volunteers, a committed team or an individual made the difference.

Expanding Your Research

Jennifer Filla is the CEO founder of the Prospect Research Institute. You can follow her on Twitter with the handle @jenfilla, where she highlights stories relevant to female donor cultivation using the hashtag #gogirlresearch. She works with universities and nonprofits, including small ones. Filla has hosted two roundtables on women's philanthropy and regularly gets the question of how to find women with giving capacity. When Filla and I spoke, she taught me about the need to move outside visible assets:

> Women don't always show the traditional markers we use in wealth ratings: Leadership on several boards, splashy gifts, steadily growing income across many years. And when we do find women of means, they may be making gifts of $1 million or $3 million to many causes, rather than $100 million in one large gift. I find that often the researcher and front-line fundraiser need to team up to learn about the woman through visits. The fundraiser can then return with clues and information, which allows the researcher to dig further.

Amy Spears echoes Filla's point. As the director of research and prospect management at the Lawrenceville School in New Jersey, Spears is a one-person research shop and brings with her 10 years of experience in research at Princeton University. Her co-ed private high school was founded in 1810 and first admitted girls in 1987. The first alumnae graduates are now in their 40s, and Spears concentrates on deepening their relationships with the school.

> Women often fly under the radar. In this small shop, I don't have the benefit of a team for research. I work with the fundraisers to gather information. They come back and share all they learned from the visits.

As Spears and I spoke, she noted her biggest take-away on tracking women:

> We must focus on the entire household, the family. Individual research does not give us the full picture. At Princeton, every part of the household is researched, analyzed and rated according to capacity by all sources, including first person conversations. When you build your information strategy with that premise, you have more context for your strategy and relationship building. Constituent systems not built with this principle are hard to fix.

The Prospect Development and Information Strategy team at the College of William & Mary focuses on household giving. As part of the advancement department's larger effort to engage women donors, PD&IS created the following team-level vision statement:

Our office will establish new policies and procedures for research and prospect management, specifically addressing how we identify, assign, track, and report on our alumnae as volunteers, leaders, and donors, directly helping our Advancement team to reach our vision of 50% representation by 2020.

PD&IS had the full support of William & Mary leaders across advancement for this vision. One of its new strategic policies has been to ensure all reports and briefings now focus equally on both members of a household, not just alumni or primary earners. PD&IS realized that when it pulled a report for a man, any of his wife's philanthropy and assets that were separate from his were not displayed and vice versa. This fact resulted in an incomplete picture of the household and led to missed opportunities for visits. The shift PD&IS made was less about the system's changes (most modern systems can combine this information), and more about the team's mindset and intentional behavior.

PD&IS also adjusted its donor tracking fields to create a more comprehensive view. Working with the information technology team, it added data fields to capture knowledge about the household beyond the direct affiliation with the university. These included:

- Employer information,
- Civic, social and professional affiliations,
- Significant awards and honors, and
- Schools children attended or were attending.

Certainly, this shift benefited all donor tracking, not just that of female prospects. Yet it was the advancement department's focus on women that moved PD&IS to make these specific changes.

When he worked for McGill University, Haider Ali paid attention to frequency of giving among female annual donors. He found that this was a strong predictor for major gift prospects. Ali noted that women's frequency of giving often is not analyzed. "Why is it that we look for those who can give a $25,000 gift one time, over the woman who is giving $1,000 a year for twenty-five years? These women are demonstrating their commitment to the university and are the ones to pay attention to."

Preeti Gill agrees with this focus on frequency. Gill is the founder of Sole Searcher Strategies, a prospect development consultancy that works primarily with social services organizations in Canada. She views women's philanthropy through the lens of a prospect research-and-development practitioner.

She blogs about her findings and tracks online resources devoted to women in business and nonprofits at www.diversitydrivendata.blog.

With permission from Gill, I include here a formula for prioritizing donors that she shared in her book *What About Women*. The formula of "Recency-Frequency-Monetary" is taken from the world of business and helps prioritize donors by assigning a numerical score for each factor. The combined score can help us see with new eyes when prioritizing women prospects:

Recency: Those who have given recently are more likely to give again.

Frequency: Donors who give frequently—regularly across years, multiple times in one year or monthly—demonstrate continued engagement and closeness. This closeness may be an indicator that you are one of their top philanthropic priorities; it is worth exploring. Don't concern yourself with the amount of each gift. It doesn't matter if she's giving $20 or $200 consistently.

Monetary: Identifies details on wealth, assets and past giving (Gill 2015).

We already use these or similar factors in other parts of our fundraising. Frequency is used for planned giving prospects. Major gift teams look at inclination, engagement and capacity. The point is to broaden your view of a woman's potential, rather than rely on one or two tags regarding capacity and current wealth. Combining your analytics in a new fashion to identify women is a small shift that can reap big results.

Both Gill and the Prospect Research Institute's Jennifer Filla pay attention to determining the giving potential of women. They shared with me some key tips:

1. **Deemphasize traditional wealth ratings.** Traditional wealth rating programs tend to find more data on men than women. The reason? Wealth screening is an aggregate of data points, and what bubbles up are those who have the most public data at this time—older, white corporate men.
   a. Gill writes in her book that 90 percent of active Wikipedia contributors are men. This points to the potential underrepresentation of women-focused information in the place we do much of our initial prospect research, the online world.
2. **The fundraisers who visit the women are your first line of information gathering.** Ask them to find out about household decision-making,

the woman's current philanthropic priorities and her network (who else does she know who might be interested in your organization?). Fundraisers can also bring back clues regarding wealth and assets. Track contact reports on each woman's record in a consistent manner.

3. **Focus on the family.** If the donor or prospect is male, turn to the women around him. Have you engaged his wife? His daughter? And if a woman is the donor or prospect, are you deepening the relationship by connecting to her family?

   a. Many daughters of high-net-worth families are part of philanthropic conversations and decisions. They've been exposed to philanthropy and might be considering how they too want to make a difference in the world.

   b. This tip aligns with research from the Women's Philanthropy Institute. The *Women Give 2013* report explored charitable giving by girls and boys. Parents who talked to their children about charity increased the likelihood of the children giving by 25 percent, regardless of the child's race, gender and age. Girls, however, were more likely to volunteer (Mesch and Osili 2013, 13–14).

4. **Learn from social media.** Filla and Gill also are beginning to glean information from social media. Gill looks at social data, particularly on Pinterest and LinkedIn, to search for women where they tend to be most social. Using these sources, you may learn about a woman's community or societal concerns, her family and friends and her networks. Include this data in her record.

5. **A final tip:** Research the woman first in the couple and place the woman first in the briefing. Gill says researching women first creates a habit that helps re-wire preconceived notions. This practice may also open insights for new approaches to the woman and her family. "I still have to re-engineer each search to incorporate information about her, fighting my own implicit bias or ease of glancing over her contributions," Gill says. "It takes time and patience to be intentional and deliberate in researching women donors."

Maintaining Accurate Records

Paying attention to a woman's name is critical. When there are errors, relationships can go awry quickly. My own name has changed over the years, and I can tell that a nonprofit doesn't really know me when they use my former married name. Accept that women's names may change for various reasons. Do they add the spouse's name and drop theirs? Have they divorced and gone back to a maiden name? Care, attention, and firsthand confirmation of how the woman wants to be addressed should be standard practice in the building of your giving pipeline and maintenance of your records.

In correspondence to a household, include the woman as a default. It is respectful and rarely inappropriate. The Indiana University Foundation houses the Women's Philanthropy Leadership Council, led by Laurie McRobbie, first lady of the University. The council had an intentional focus on the issue of salutation. In 2013, they conducted a campus survey to benchmark university-wide practices in addressing correspondence to women recipients. The analysis found inconsistencies in salutations as well as the exclusion at times of the woman, possibly even when she made the gift from her own funds. The foundation issued a formal request to colleagues across campus to include women in all correspondence. The letter noted the importance of women's giving in today's world and the need to have acknowledgments recognize their influence and generosity.

In addition, the university instituted a new policy for addressing couples and writing salutations. Now, the school uses stacked names in recipient addresses (first name, above the second name, above the address). If she's the alumna and he isn't, her name goes first. If they're both alumni, whoever graduated first is listed at the top. In cases where there is no difference, the foundation asked development officers to be alert to who their primary contact is, although in many cases his name will go first. Salutations follow the same order principles as addresses, and the university uses "Ms." or "Dr." as the standard honorifics for women. Names are listed separately (e.g., "Dear Mr. Smith and Ms. Smith"). Donors can request more traditional address forms and salutations, but the university no longer defaults to them. All of these changes resonated positively with alumnae. The university now rarely receives complaints on this matter and believes they have made a permanent cultural shift on respectfully addressing women.

Unlocking Women's Networks

As you consider creative new approaches to prospect identification, learn about women's networks. Researching and engaging their networks can be a successful method to grow your donor pipeline and gifts. The Tahirih Justice Center had great success with this approach in a major campaign.

Tahirih is a national nonprofit that has answered more than 22,000 pleas for help from immigrant women and girls fleeing violence since 1997. Through free legal services, social services case management, policy advocacy and training and education, Tahirih protects these courageous women and girls, helping them attain the most basic of human rights—to live in safety and with dignity. Tahirih's annual budget is $7.5 million. In 2013, the organization embarked on a five-year, $10 million expansion campaign to open two new U.S. offices, increasing the number of women and girls it served by 250 percent, doubling both its policy advocacy outreach and training and education efforts with first-responders.

The transformative power of networked high-net-worth women was a game-changer in Tahirih's campaign. It started with one couple already committed to the mission. In early 2015, the wife of the couple decided she wanted to introduce Tahirih to others. I'll call her Ana. She held a retreat at a high-end spa in California's Napa Valley for 10 to 12 close friends with financial capacity. Ana hosted the retreat, paid for all the lodging and food and did all the organizing. Tahirih's CEO joined them for the weekend, got to know the women socially and led several formal presentations about the work, immersing them in client experiences and the organization's programs and arming them as spokeswomen for the organization. Throughout the weekend, Ana's friends tried to help pay for food and the massage packages that she gifted. Ana responded that they should save their money for Tahirih. At the end of the weekend, they came together to hear about the $10 million campaign and the need for a committed group to help raise money. Ana and Tahirih's CEO handed them pledge forms and asked them to indicate both what they could give personally and what they could help raise. The women called themselves "the Soul Sisters" and committed to take ownership of fundraising for the campaign. With the energy and network birthed by this group, Tahirih received over $1 million in new campaign funding over the next two years.

How did this happen? One woman at the first Soul Sister retreat decided to make Tahirih one of her philanthropic priorities. She and her husband hosted a fundraising event for Tahirih in their beautiful home in Southern California. She set a goal of $100,000 for the event and created her own committee. The committee did most of the work, with some support from Tahirih. In April 2016, the event raised $125,000. "Nana," a friend of one of the Soul Sisters, was so moved by what she learned about Tahirih that she flew to the organization's Virginia headquarters for a site visit. At that meeting, Nana decided to give her first gift, $90,000. She then hosted her own fundraising dinner, which raised over $100,000 and introduced 100 more people to Tahirih.

Tahirih stayed in touch with the attendees of these key events, the majority of whom were women. It tracked all the relationships carefully. First-time guests became advocates for the organization, and many brought their friends together in their own homes to continue raising awareness of the organization's work and needs. These events were social in nature—the women delighted in seeing each other or meeting for the first time, as well as connecting to the cause. The stated goal was always to partner to help spread the word, raise awareness and give what was possible. Each event not only raised money but also added to the snowballing Tahirih network. Soon after the first Soul Sister retreat, high-net-worth women up and down the California coast were supporting Tahirih.

This network transformed Tahirih. The organization found a new niche of prospects it would never have been able to identify through traditional research. The new support allowed the organization to open its San Francisco office, with a bonded group of women deeply committed to sustaining the site. These woman are already planning a large fundraiser for 2018, as well as a third Soul Sisters retreat.

Just as important, the women were changed by their involvement. Take, for example, Nana. Nana took bold, decisive actions—flying across the country to learn more about Tahirih and making a significant first gift to the organization. You may be surprised to learn that, at first, Nana felt nervous about stepping into the role of an advocate for Tahirih. Although confident in giving her own gift, how could she ask others to give? How could she speak in compelling terms about the important work of the organization? Over the past two years, with support from her fellow Soul Sisters and the Tahirih staff, she became a confident leader and powerful voice for Tahirih. Now she does not hesitate to have direct conversations and ask people to provide support, financial and otherwise. She makes leadership requests, using both the facts and her own stories about helping the women and girls in desperate situations. Nana became a member of the Tahirih expansion campaign committee and regularly shares how her life was transformed due to her involvement. Her efforts to grow Tahirih's funding and impact have led to personal growth and new skills.

Metrics

The strategies you choose to widen your pipeline of women prospects and donors will necessarily dictate the metrics you track as measures of success. Here are a few examples to help you contemplate what you will monitor:

- Fundraisers
  - Track if your fundraisers are sharing information with researchers.
  - Instill a visit protocol to learn about household decision-making and household philanthropy.
  - Ask about and record what she cares about.
  - Ask about and record her relationships and networks outside of her family that are also connected, or might be, to your mission.
- Constituent management
  - Create and track women-inclusive reporting.
    - Review regularly the accuracy of women's names.
    - Are all reports pulled with a gender breakdown?
    - Do women come first on briefings?
    - Are women soft-credited in a household if a man signed a check but both names are on the check?
    - Are women included in acknowledgment letters by default?
    - Track frequency of gifts from women.
- Research
  - Track Google or other alerts that can provide additional information on women prospects and donors.
    - Tune in to what they care about through what they say, write and express through the social handles they use online.
  - Track household philanthropy and next-generation interests.
  - Review the archive of contact reports in the database for your top male donors to unearth and separate out details they may have shared about the women in their lives.

CHAPTER TAKE-AWAYS

- Keep in mind that unconscious stories about women might be entrenched in your data system or in the ways that you have employed it to date. Find ways to make your constituent-management system and its use more female-friendly.
- Recognize that your current research methods might uncover more information about men than women.
  - Partner with others in your organization to keep learning about women.
  - Look to alternative sources for information.
- Design new ways to learn and record information about women prospects and donors.
- Attend to entire household giving as well as to the individuals in that home.
- Add frequency of giving when prioritizing women donors.
- Follow the network around your women donors—more prospects may be in plain view.

Chapter 9

INSPIRE

"I want to hear what is happening, not just what funding is needed."
—Interview with alumna

Overview

This chapter is about communication. Instead of calling it the "Inform" chapter, like the traditional donor cycle, I choose to call it "Inspire." You want your communications to inspire your constituents, including women, to partner with your mission.

We've learned from the Women's Philanthropy Institute that high-networth men and women have different motivations for giving. More women than men give when:

- there is an alignment with political or philosophical beliefs (connection to values);
- they are engaged (volunteering, on a board); and
- something unexpected arises (disasters, short-term challenges or opportunities).

Empathy is at the core of these motivational differences. WPI's report, "How and Why Women Give," demonstrated that women tend to be more empathetic and altruistic than men. This difference has implications for their giving, as those characteristics directly motivate their philanthropy. "When women give, they tend to express a desire to help others, whereas men tend to focus on the benefits that come from being charitable" (Mesch et al. 2015a, 5).

Empathy is an emotion of caring. It is the ability to understand others' feelings. Extended into philanthropy, it is a driver to have impact and to create better outcomes for those being served because one can really see their needs and imagine their feelings. Empathy drives an individual to not just make a transactional gift, but to be involved. A woman often looks for more than information to learn about an organization and how she can be involved. Information is logical. And logic is important to make decisions. However, additional words and stories that connect to empathy, demonstrate impact, show involvement and let women see themselves reflected in an organization's mission will resonate and deepen potential conversations and relationships.

To inspire women to connect, pay attention to three key questions:

- What do women see when they look at your organization?
- How does your organization communicate with women?
- How do you as an individual communicate with women?

My book provides many examples to help you choose the communication actions that will work with your unique culture and women stakeholders.

Design

What do women see when they look at your organization?

Your organization has a public face made up of your marketing materials, your website, your social media presence and your leadership. Do women see themselves and what they care about in this external face? Do they see an equal number of women and men in your photos? In the stories you tell about donors and volunteers? Among your leadership profiles?

Consider conducting a baseline evaluation of what women see now when they look at you. One tool is an audit of the ways you present your organization to your stakeholders. It need not be a formal audit, nor a review of the whole organization if it is a large one. You might start with the development department's marketing collateral, including appeals, newsletters, reports and stewardship materials. The "who" might be an intern, a task force of women stakeholders, a team from your communications staff or a pro-bono contract with an outside communications team. You want someone who can objectively look through the lens of a woman and report back on the types and frequency of visuals and language presented. Note the number of:

- Photos of women vs. men,
- Headlines about women and their accomplishments,
- Awards given to women, and
- Stories about women volunteers, donors and networks.

Your quantitative baseline review can also look at the leadership. Reflect on whether the frequency you find is proportional to your stakeholder population now and in the likely future. Note the number of:

- Women on the board or other volunteer leadership groups, and
- Women on the leadership staff.

After this initial assessment, you may wish to conduct a communications survey and/or interviews with representative women stakeholders. Expand on the information garnered in the above audit by asking these women how they view your organization, what they value and their current impressions of the organization's leadership and work. If you choose to design a survey, the "who" for this mechanism needs the skill to create a statistically useful tool and the ability to analyze the results. That person may be in-house, a volunteer or a paid contractor. Some potential questions might include:

- What resonates most with you about our organization? Do you see that in our materials?
- As you think of us, what words, visuals or feelings come to mind?
- Where do you go to learn about our organization? To your peers? Your network? The website? Social media? Newsletters?
- Have you recently told anyone else about our organization? If so, what information did you share?
- What do you wish to see more of in our communications?

How does your organization communicate with women?

Georgetown University linguist and best-selling author Deborah Tannen has investigated gendered communication styles for more than 20 years. She argues that men and women have different ways of speaking because they grow up and are acculturated in different environments. How they played in their early years and were treated at school, and the consequences of being perceived as "bossy" or "assertive," all influence the ways women converse and understand conversations.

Gender differences in communication begin at a very early age, as Tannen (2010) discovered in one study. Observing 4-year-olds at play, she found that boys often sit next to each other and talk while looking straight-ahead. Picture men at a sporting event. Girls often pull up a chair facing one another, make eye contact and then talk.

Later in life, women communicate to build rapport much more than men and often emphasize "we" over "I." Men and women can walk away from the same exchange asking different questions. As Tannen explains, "he might wonder, 'Did that conversation put me in a one-up or a one-down position?' whereas she might wonder 'Did it bring us closer or push us farther apart?'"

Our communication about women and to women will resonate more clearly with them if we note the "we," the group effort. Language that allows women to feel and envision connections is more compelling than "just the facts, ma'am."

As discussed in Chapter 1, this greater tendency toward connection or empathy motivates women donors. René Bekkers and Pamala Wiepking reviewed over 500 scholarly papers on charitable giving and found there were eight mechanisms that drove philanthropic behavior: (1) awareness of need; (2) solicitation; (3) costs and benefits; (4) altruism; (5) reputation; (6) psychological benefits; (7) values; and (8) efficacy. From these eight they found that two mattered most for women to give: personal values, or a sense of needing to care for others, and psychological benefits or feelings that create a "warm glow" or "empathetic joy" (Bekkers and Wiepking 2011, 924).

Is your organization's communication style purely informational, or does it also allow the reader to recognize interpersonal connections, potentially leading them to involvement? We know that men think primarily with logic, using their brain's left hemisphere. Women are much more likely to also engage the other hemisphere when making decisions (Goldman 2017). They need logic to make the final decision, but what they hear or read must also resonate intuitively with them. Are you using written language that connects with women's sense of empathy?

These are not black and white questions that can be answered quickly. As I've written before, we are opening up our curiosity to reflect on what we've often done unconsciously.

The presentation of your organizational needs can be adapted by connecting to what women care about. Here is a quote from a woman at one focus group:

> I started off giving [the organization] small gifts, and gave regularly, even if small amounts. When I had more affluence, I gave more. I wondered if anyone noticed and would talk to me about my giving. Finally, a male volunteer who knew my husband came to visit. He asked me if I'd like to help [the organization] at a bigger level and would I fund a scholarship. I said that would be boring. Over a period, he got to know me, including my interest in early childhood education. One day he described the need for and impact of a new childcare center on site. I said yes and was happy to give that larger gift.

This donor describes the joy she felt about giving after she was offered an opportunity that matched her values and would provide clear impact.

Doesn't that describe how all philanthropy should be? Of course! All donors prefer to be met, known and connected to issues they care about. I am a strong proponent of relationship-based philanthropy. I was lucky to be mentored in this approach and am worried that today's fast-paced fundraising often forsakes the long-term relationship for the quick gift to achieve this year's goal. But this book is about what we can adjust today to grow women's philanthropy. If we know that women are more connected to empathy and care for others, then it is crucial to communicate with words and visuals that resonate.

I'm not suggesting that you re-work all your communications. I do encourage you to think deeply about how your communication style may or may not be reaching women. Reflect on these questions:

- Do you highlight collaboration and connection?
  - When you tell a story about a gift that came in, do you include all decision-makers, even if one is not the obvious stakeholder (volunteer, donor, alumni/alumnae) for your organization?
  - When you write about the impact that a gift made, do you describe how the entire village (donor, program staff, etc.) helped make it happen?
  - Do you search for pictures and stories about collaboration and strong peer relationships where the group has a social connection, as well as a focus on creating impact?

- Do you tell stories about the benefits of connecting to other volunteers and donors from your organization, even if there is no immediate financial benefit for you? These stories might be about netweaving that allowed one of your volunteer leaders to switch careers, take on a new volunteer role for a case she is passionate about or learn new health information that positively impacted her family.
- Do impact statements appeal to a variety of giving motivations?
  - Do you tell stories about the impact of support—volunteer or financial—that solved problems and affected lasting change? Do these stories include the qualitative effect of the outcome as well as the quantitative facts?
- Do you tell women's stories?
  - When a woman chooses to make a significantly higher gift than in the past, do you ask her why? Then, with her permission, do you highlight not just the gift, but her thought process and how she came to her decision?
  - When you showcase a woman donor or volunteer, do you also mention her network and the other ways she shares her interests and builds support for your mission?
  - How often do you interview and then highlight women volunteers and donors with questions that help them share their values, connections and process?

As part of the incremental improvements to your communications, interview or survey your women stakeholders to test if certain materials resonate. Adapt a few general outreach pieces at a time. Remember, when you try to connect with women the same way you do with men, they may get turned off. However, when you connect with men in the ways women prefer, men will respond. If you slowly adapt your communication style with this in mind, you'll enjoy the long-term benefit of resonating with a majority of your stakeholders.

Teaching your front-line fundraisers about the power of adapting language to appeal to female prospects and donors, and training them to do so, can serve as another mechanism for change in your organization. I don't mean just holding another diversity training, because we know that those don't stick. When we learn something but do not put it into practice, nothing fundamentally changes. However, there is hands-on training offered today that puts participants in the shoes of "the other" and offers practice speaking and receiving communication that fits.

How do you as an individual communicate with women?

Just as it's important how your organization communicates with women, the approaches noted above are also critical in one-to-one communications. Whether using a personalized letter or email, a meeting or an invitation to join an event or group, we want to choose words and images that capture the attention, feelings and values of the woman we are addressing. We also want to avoid concepts that do not resonate, such as deadlines and funding goals. However, successful communication comes down to more than using the right words to ask for participation or a gift. What do you know about the woman you are writing to or visiting? How can you find out what her values are and what she cares about?

Women want to feel connected with an organization before giving, *and* they want the individuals in the organization to connect personally to them. In many focus groups, I hear quotes like this:

- My motivation to give comes down to personal connection and being involved. Then I'll listen to an ask.
- The important thing when asking me for a gift is the relationship quality.
- What are the ways to get women to give? Give us individual attention (not just to our husbands) and tell us about the need and impact before asking.

Relationship quality—what is that? Perhaps you took the same communication courses I did that taught us that true communication is less about what words are spoken and far more about the body language, mood and tone of the speaker. We connect first to the energy and intent of the person speaking to us and then to the conversation. Relationship quality starts with truly feeling your own curiosity and projecting a mood of connection and an authentic interest in learning about who is right in front of us. How often do we start donor meetings with a scan of a person's home or office, a few quick questions about the view or the pictures we see, and then quickly move into a conversation about why we are meeting? Everyone's time is precious, and we *do* want to be respectful about the time we spend with prospective donors and get to the heart of the conversation. I believe there is a different approach, one that can build relationships in every encounter.

I propose that we "blend" with all our donors, particularly with women.

What is blending? There is a myth that fundraisers need to be nice, listen to the donor and then follow the donor's interests. We talk about being "donor-centered" but let's be honest: We're all working under pressure. We have goals to hit, money to raise, worries about work reviews and large portfolios of donors to cultivate. This can lead to a perceptible disconnect between what we're actually thinking (can today's visit further my goals?) and the impression we'd like to make (listen to the donor). Whenever we experience this disconnect, people feel it—no matter how we may try to hide it.

Relational communication is about first aligning with our overarching commitments. Immediate pressures sometimes overshadow commitments to build partnerships with our donors. Align first with your own desire for a sustained relationship. I can safely assume that you care deeply about your long-term commitment to help achieve your organization's mission by growing a deep pool of loyal supporters. Once you're standing firm in this bigger commitment, you can then connect with the person in front of you. What does she value? What are her concerns? How would she like to support your organization and help you with your big commitment? How can you help her achieve her commitments? Blending means being firmly committed to our own, larger mission while also being open to the donor or prospect right in front of us. Blending encourages us to be transparent about our own commitment and listen deeply to the concerns of our prospective women donors.

What does blending look like? "Ms. Samuel, I care deeply for [our organization] and wake up every morning thinking about how I can help generate support for its amazing programs and clients. I know you care as well. What is important to you? What are your values? I'd like to understand what you care about and see if we can fulfill your values within our mission."

This opener does not take much time away from your meeting, yet it leads to a totally different conversation. Start with a clear statement regarding what you care about and you are transparent about the fact that you are a fundraiser and have a commitment to raising revenue. Follow with a clear curiosity about the person in front of you, rather than launching into X program description or Y naming opportunity.

This approach can be used in every conversation or email or letter—not just the first ones. When you are writing back about a program she's expressed interest in, you can also ask if the program's values and impact match what she cares about. When you notice she is worried about how to make the gift, you can gently probe her concerns and in doing so, perhaps learn more about her values and key motivations. When she wonders on a call about how this gift can be leveraged, you can explore what she means by that, how she has done this in the past and who she might share this with in her network. When you hear her answer to one of your questions, follow up by saying, "Tell me more." This simple phrase allows her to deepen and further clarify what is important and why.

In essence, every interaction with a prospect or donor is an opportunity to build or deepen a trusted relationship with open-ended, curious questions that allow her to reflect and share. Adding such questions throughout a relationship won't take more time, but it will open a richness that women, and most donors, prefer. Everyone is busy, but it is rare that someone will not share what is meaningful to them and what they hope to do with their resources. In fact, many of us crave these conversations. As James Gilmore and Joseph Pine explain in their book, *Authenticity: What Consumers Really Want*:

> Today participating in meaningful experiences represents the largest unmet needs of Americans, more precious than economic capital: religion, country, art, and family and education, these are the resources that are literally priceless, from which we draw distinctions regarding our purposes in life. (Gilmore and Pine 2007, 76)

Metrics

Metrics for your implementation will follow your choice of goals. After you fully understand your current state of communications to and about women, you can then design benchmarks for change and report against those. I've listed examples of metrics below.

- Track over time what women see when they look at your organization:
  - Monitor the number of (a) photos of women vs. men, (b) headlines about women and their accomplishments, (c) awards given to women and (d) stories about women volunteers, donors and networks in marketing and development materials.
  - Conduct regular surveys or focus groups to see changes in women's opinions in response to your efforts. For example, you can ask stakeholders to rate articles in your print media as low-, medium- or high-value on an annual basis.
- Track over time how your organization communicates with women:
  - Number of communications materials that intentionally (a) highlight collaboration and connection, (b) describe impact both quantitatively and qualitatively and (c) tell women stakeholders' stories.

- Number of communications materials created or edited in response to direct feedback from women focus groups, interviews and surveys.
- Number of staff members trained in adapting language to appeal to female prospects and donors.
- Number of donor visits in which frontline fundraisers self-report implementing this training.
- Staff performance review ratings on adapting language.

Measuring the change over time in the strength of one-on-one relationships is more difficult to pin down. Nevertheless, after training those who interact with your women prospects in the blending approach, it is valuable to establish metrics around these changes. James Hodge's book, *Philanthropy & Relationships*, asks an important question: "If philanthropy is all about relationships, then why do metrics only measure money?" Hodge offers useful examples for quantifying the strength of relationships:

Likert Scale questions can be developed that help monitor and chart the relationship metrics of our encounters, engagement, and experiences with donors/prospects. Such a series of weighted questions can determine how skilled a development officer is at creating and strengthening relationship.

Two master key questions of importance are as follows: First, what is my relationship equity with this benefactor? How do I resonate with this donor or prospect and what is our level of mutual trust?

0	1	2	3	4	5
New/Weak					Mature/Strong

Second, what is the institutional relationship quotient with this benefactor? Am I strengthening the ties between this potential donor and our organization, our leaders and our mission?

0	1	2	3	4	5
Little/Weak					Substantial/Strong

(Hodge 2011, 9).

We all know the adage, "What gets measured gets managed." Simply having questions like these in place as part of your donor tracking protocol can enhance awareness and create changed behavior. Questions about the strength of donor relationships can be inserted into a performance review between a manager and a fundraiser, or used as a self-review.

To assist in your strategic design, I've included, with permission from William & Mary, an overview of the top actions and metrics their communications team chose. This example may be helpful for your own work.

Objective
- Transform the College of William & Mary's current communications to be more representative of, and oriented to, women and underrepresented groups.

Key Actions
- Conduct a communications audit, looking at all the ways William & Mary communicates about and to women and underrepresented groups.
- Showcase alumnae equally across William & Mary's communications.
- Highlight successful William & Mary alumnae to the wider campus community.
- Train development staff, alumni association staff, the Internal Advisory Committee, the 100th Anniversary Committee, the campaign cabinet, foundation trustees and key fundraising volunteers specifically around inclusive language and communications oriented to women.
- Showcase the impact of giving.

Suggested Metrics
- Number of women nominated for Alumni Association Medallions or other alumni awards, number of honorary degrees given to women and number of women featured as the commencement speaker.
- Number of women to appear in alumni communications (e.g., alumni newsletters, magazine, etc.) as well as the prominence of the story.
- Increase over time the stewardship efforts using student involvement against pre-established baseline.
- Progress and improvements against initial audit results, tracked by additional audits to ensure changes are being made.

CHAPTER TAKE-AWAYS

Women will look at your organization and read or listen to your words carefully to decide if they want to get involved. Many will care if women are reflected equally. They will listen for report *and* rapport. They'll want the data as well as an understanding of context and connections that are part of your impact in the world.

How does your organization look to a woman contemplating support?

- Consider a quantitative audit to learn if you are even-handed in what you present.
- Consider asking your women stakeholders what resonates, or not, and why.

How well do you communicate to men and women in your public messaging?

- Train your team to understand that men and women may have different communications styles.
- Emphasize language that showcases empathy and connections, in addition to reporting facts.

Does your individual communication with women connect to their concerns in addition to organizational needs?

- Consistently ask about and check in that you are meeting her values and questions.
- Consider a performance benchmark on the relationship quality with her.

Chapter 10

INVOLVE

"The more I know, the more hands-on I will become with the cause, and the more I can see where I can help."
—Interview with alumna

Overview

What is involvement for women? It certainly is no longer the 1950s model of volunteering significant hours each week while the children are in school. Today, women are often multi-tasking, dividing their time with work, children, aging parents and the many relationships in their lives. Yet the longing to join with others to make a difference beyond home and work is still palpable. Linda Paulson, vice president of philanthropic engagement at Washington Area Women's Foundation, expressed the importance of this desire to women's giving. "When I connect to one woman about an issue, she connects to her network and helps build a team to address the issue. Women want to be part of something bigger than themselves and design joint success."

We know that engagement is a key motivator for women's philanthropy. In its 2015 literature review of women's philanthropy, the Women's Philanthropy Institute described studies of "gender socialization and social role theory" that help us understand "why women may derive greater satisfaction and rewards from volunteering":

From an early age women are socialized into more helping, nurturing, and caring roles, demonstrating empathy for others, while men are socialized into heroic and chivalrous roles that are more task-oriented, which leads women to volunteer more . . . Incorporating both social learning theory and biological differences, Wymer (2011) finds that women prefer helping people in need and organizations that help infants and children, while men prefer volunteer roles that include some level of risk-taking. Similarly, women prefer to volunteer for organizations that are people-oriented, emphasize community, and value volunteer input. (Mesch, et al. 2015a, 33)

Past women's philanthropy programs echo this research. In almost every program, women gravitated to activities that allowed them to connect meaningfully—to each other, the beneficiaries and the organization. Sloane Davidson, a member of the WPI Advisory Council, said at the March 2017 WPI Symposium, "Women prefer to convene, collaborate, and find community to catalyze change." Women have an inherent ability and desire to network and leverage their network to learn, share and use combined resources (time, skills and money) to make a difference.

Before we design meaningful ways to involve women in your organization, let's look at what women say they prefer when they are choosing how to be engaged.

More Than Money

As we see in today's headlines, women are raising their voices after lifetimes of not being heard or respected. They've also not been heard in the nonprofit sector. Women regularly insist they are more than checkbooks, yet many feel this point is ignored.

Women understand the importance of resourcing, versus just fundraising. Resourcing is reviewing the whole system to better determine what assistance would be most beneficial, whether money, time, information, in-kind support, network, community building, etc. Fundraising that does not encompass this broader definition of support might simply redistribute money from those who have it to where it's lacking. Many women look beyond dollars, preferring to create sustainable solutions. "[Being a] 'philanthropist' had to be redefined in my mind for me, which is more than just financing and funding," one participant in a WPI survey of high-net-worth women said. "It's actually being engaged in the work and putting in time and effort and care" (O'Connor et al. 2018, 27).

In *Women & Philanthropy: Boldly Shaping a Better World*, Sondra Shaw-Hardy and Martha A. Taylor (2010, 132) list additional resources women provide:

- Intellectual capital
- Nonhierarchical management
- Experience and a new perspective
- Listening skills
- Entrepreneurial approach
- Capacity to deliver change
- Consensus building
- Volunteer experience
- Nurturing and altruism

When women believe they are welcomed as more than checkbooks, they feel respected, heard, valued and trusted. These feelings can lead to a willingness to speak up and give voice to what is not working and what they view as possible. If you treat all donors, and women in particular, as whole people who have a number of gifts to offer your organization, you gain so much more than funds. You gain their connections, expertise, creativity and willingness to dig in with you. It is at this point that the magic of women's engagement and philanthropy begins.

Given the many resources women bring to the table, what ways are you inviting in all the resources that women have to offer? Do you track the many resources she is providing? How do you intentionally acknowledge all that a woman may be doing for your organization, including but also beyond financial support?

Networks

For millennia, women have come together in networks to address challenges. Regardless of the country or culture, there are gatherings of women focused on local politics, the environment, water quality, maternal and child health, spirituality, books, parenting and a myriad of other concerns. Jean Shinoda Bolen, the founder of the Millionth Circle Movement, said in an interview that she saw that a new way of human relating, "tend and befriend" rather than "fight or flight," is spreading rapidly. Women are leading the way (Gaia 2017).

In a 2011 report on women's giving networks, the Center on Philanthropy at Indiana University notes:

These "networks" create opportunities for members to become knowledgeable about their communities, take an active interest in social and political issues, gain greater confidence in their own abilities, acquire social and civic skills, and learn how to listen and trust others and work collaboratively. (2011, 2)

Recognizing the importance of networks is useful for two reasons. First, many women will choose to become involved collaboratively with others when tackling an issue, rather than work alone. They may want to be part of something bigger than themselves. Second, others may be willing to enthusiastically share their involvement with members of their network. They may bring additional women to events or engage them in your programs. This can grow your pipeline.

Given the importance of a woman's network:

- How do you learn about a woman's network?
- Do you have strategies to involve the individual *and* her network?
- What questions are you asking to discern if a woman wants to be involved individually, or is interested in collaboration?
- How do you support her to share her involvement with her network?

Connection to Other Women

A key component within women's networks is the participants' connection to each other. The College of William & Mary discovered that personal connections between their alumnae, and with alumni, were *the* primary source of engagement with the school. These connected groups were often organized by the alumnae themselves. One woman shared, "I stay connected to William & Mary friends within my sorority—this is our tenth year of annual gatherings." Another maintained her relationship with the school through "personal communication with William & Mary friends. We travel in our social groups for athletic events throughout New England."

The importance of personal connections is true for all donors—we are more likely to listen to our trusted friends and colleagues than strangers. This is particularly true for women. Women have gathered for centuries, often for survival, to share and support. From quilting bees to today's powerful moms' groups on Facebook, women build communities where they can learn from each other, cry together, cheer each other and attend to relationships they can trust.

Given the special bond women have with each other, how do you provide space and time for women to connect and share with each other when they are gathered to help your cause? Respecting this behavior yields benefits of loyalty, referrals and the creativity that comes from the open space of connection.

Life Stages

From listening to many focus groups, I have learned that women prefer engagement that recognizes their life cycles:

> "I was not involved until 10 years ago because of my career and babies. Now I am very involved."
>
> "When I became aware of [XX organization], I was working full time and the events were in the city after work. It just didn't work for me—the timing didn't fit with my life."
>
> "My engagement has a life cycle or rhythm. Make it OK for me to check in and out. There are times for leadership roles and times I need to draw back."

These life stages can make it difficult for organizations to maintain a prospect pool for women leaders. The task requires care and attention. When Haider Ali was doing donor analytics at McGill University, he said the school had "a leaky pipeline for women leadership candidates because women's connections to McGill shifted based on their life obligations." A volunteer at William & Mary said: "I was asked to be on the Business School Board. I said no at that time, and I never heard from them again. Just because 'no' comes at a certain time does not mean for all times. Just keep asking until there is the right fit and time."

Learning about a woman's time capacity at different stages in her life is important in devising appropriate cultivation strategies. For instance:

- How do you stay in touch throughout the different stages of her life?
- How do you schedule events? Are you mindful of not scheduling night meetings for women with small children, or day meetings for women with demanding careers?
- How do you learn about and track the various key stages? Do you record key life shifts such as career changes, marriage, childcare years, eldercare years, grandchildren, retirement and any combination of these phases?

High Impact

As noted in Chapter 1, involved women often prefer high-impact over high-profile roles. Nannerl O. Keohane, former president of both Wellesley College and Duke University, spoke to a focus group I attended in 2013. She noted that women are more likely to get directly involved in meaningful volunteer work to solve problems and create new solutions, rather than to assume high-profile roles with titles and visibility. Keohane shared examples of female students choosing to be second in command on a leadership council and helping get things done, instead of running for the leadership seat. It can be a tendency of women to focus more on helping others, she said, than on one's own ego.

This description was grounded by quotes from women in other focus groups. One said, "I'm better as a follower than a leader, and title is not important. I get involved because of self-satisfaction and feeling good about making a difference in something I believe in."

Certainly, there are many women who have shrugged off this early socialization to combine their care for others with owning their leadership visibility and influence. For the sake of this book, however, I want to point out that women's early socialization must be taken into account by fundraisers; don't make assumptions.

Knowing that many women are less interested in titles, how might you approach her to join a Board or Council? What different conversation might you have to discern her interest? How might you look for leadership candidates differently, knowing that women with the qualities you need may have chosen engagement roles without titles, or stepped back for a period?

Design

How might you create meaningful engagement that honors women's preferences, avoids being resource-intensive for staff and leads to growth in women's leadership and philanthropy?

Below are many ideas, from short engagement opportunities to longer-term strategies. I know from what women have shared over the years that long and complex engagement is not always required. Women appreciate what I call "Short Shots" that fit into their schedule and allow them to create impact on their own or with a group. Many of the ideas below cut across departmental silos and work responsibilities. Bear in mind that the specific actions listed were chosen based on the culture and moment in time for each organization. Each then built the unique stakeholder group needed to achieve its goals, such as organizational leadership, communications, women volunteers to design the activity, and so forth. Hopefully these examples provide starter fuel for what might work for your unique culture and vision.

Short-Shots

Many organizations have time-limited but meaningful ways to involve women. As already noted, these ideas can work for all donors, but they are particularly meaningful for women.

- Asking for her opinion or expertise on an issue, and following up with the results.
  - One alumna of USF who was a leader in manufacturing was very helpful when a professor wanted to enhance how he was teaching about supply-chain operations. She provided her expertise as well as some other connections and context to consider.
  - This simple and respectful request speaks volumes—you see her, you value her thoughts, you want to listen and learn from her.
  - Ways to gather her input can be as broad as participating in a focus group or survey, or individualized to a meeting.
- Reaching out during important life transitions.
  - Dorothy Heinrichs, senior associate director of leadership initiatives for the Geisel School of Medicine at Dartmouth College and Dartmouth-Hitchcock health system, shared how meaningful it was to a donor when she called on the anniversary of the spouse's death to simply check in.
  - Heinrichs also made a point to call donors after the 2016 national elections, regardless of how they might have voted. She simply asked, "How are you?" and listened.
  - The personal touch is priceless. The receiver feels seen and remembered, which builds loyalty and a desire to stay involved. This is part of fundraising training, but too often it's not implemented.
- Inviting her to host a gathering of those in her network who might care about your mission.
  - McGill University had a very shallow pipeline of women leaders and major donors. It invited women leaders already engaged with the university to host dinners in their homes for their friends and colleagues

who had gone to McGill. The table discussion was part catching up with each other, part talking about McGill's latest vision and strategies. After salons in three different cities, the pipeline had grown significantly with many more women willing to stay in touch or become engaged with the university.

- ○ This engagement opportunity is also "local"—something a woman donor can do in her home or a at community restaurant. There is a higher likelihood of involvement if the event is easy and fits into her life.
- Designing community service events.
  - ○ The Minneapolis chapter of the American Red Cross invited families and groups of friends to come together on a Saturday morning to create preparedness kits to be provided to schools in the community.
  - ○ Women are open to engaging their children when possible. Philanthropic parents want to pass on these values to their children (Mesch and Osili 2013, 4).
  - ○ This idea taps into the women's community, her desire to be engaged with her community, as well as her preference to do meaningful work.

Based on your vision and intention for growing women's support, you will come up with your own "short shots." Remember these do not need to be time-intensive. In fact, light touches are optimal during times when the woman is consumed with other aspects of life. The goal is to learn more about the woman (even a meaningful conversation is engagement), ask for her input and how she prefers to connect, and find ways to include her family, network and community if she so desires.

Creating Community

Events that create community can include stand-alone, one-off activities, larger series of repeated meetings or annual meetings or symposia with inspiring speakers and break-out sessions. Some institutions also set up intimate lunches or dinners in their regions to connect to women and their networks. Below are some examples:

- M.I.A.M.I. Women at Miami University in Ohio hosts an annual Women's Leadership Symposium. The group connects alumni (men and women), campus leaders and student groups to learn about and discuss relevant topics. Keynote speakers across the years have included actress

Geena Davis, as well as noted journalists Nicholas Kristof and Sheryl WuDunn, who together wrote the book *Half the Sky* about the importance of women.

- Tiffany Circle members at the American Red Cross gather annually in key cities. Past agendas in Washington included dinners at the State Department, a briefing by the Department of Homeland Security and briefings by Red Cross leaders.
- Community is created across generations within Women 4 Change at Hamilton Community Foundation. Members' ages range from millennials to the World War II generation. The Hamilton Community Foundation's Sheree Meredith consistently hears about the quality of discussion that happens when a 70-year-old and 30-year-old are sharing experiences and concerns, and together coming up with new insights.

These events allow for meaningful connections with organizational leadership, inspirational speakers and the impactful work unfolding. In addition, time is often allotted for the women to connect to each other. Attendees feel they are part of a special community and often walk away feeling inspired, or at least more informed.

In addition to creating community among the women and with the organization, events can connect stakeholders to beneficiaries.

N Street Village, a Washington, D.C. nonprofit, empowers homeless and low-income women to claim a higher quality of life. It provides shelter, meals, health support and job training. NSV has a clear focus of asking its supporters for all resources, not just finances. One group of annual donors, the Ambassadors, are primarily women. The Ambassadors also volunteer. One activity was a community dinner—cooking for, serving, talking to and even singing with the 42 residents. Thanks to these dinners, each Ambassador knows the impact she makes.

The Jewish Federations of North America hosts "Heart to Heart" mission trips to Israel for the federations. The trips are an intense four days, scheduled during weekdays so there is no weekend time away from the family. The trips are for women only and are designed to strengthen bonds to each other, the federation's work and women in Israel. Women get the chance to learn about the impact of programs on the ground. Women who have gone on these trips talk about how connecting, emotional, enlightening and thought-provoking the experience was for them. Beth Mann, JFNA's vice president of institutional advancement, shared with me the inclusiveness and long-reaching impact of this unique program:

> Our trips are meant for any woman; we only suggest a gift of $500 to their local federation and do not solicit for money on the trip. Yet despite this, most women begin giving more after the trip. Many go from not giving at all to giving $5,000 or more. The power of the trip is in the group and showcasing the work. They come face to face with our work, and they fall in love. Once they fall in love, our mission is theirs forever.

How might you create experiences that help women fall in love with your programs? Ask the women. Many of the ideas above came from women. And women who help generate ideas often raise their hands to help. As Mann witnesses over and over again, once a woman is involved, she is willing to volunteer to help implement.

Leadership

Many efforts to expand women's philanthropy include the commitment to grow women's leadership. When it's a good fit, being a leader for an organization is a very personal and high impact way for a woman to be involved. Some design components include:

- *Ask her to become a leader.* I heard this over and over in focus groups: "I've not been asked." One focus-group participant said, "I just stepped down as Board Chair for [another organization]. I had no prior association with the organization, but I was asked. We don't ask enough." Our failure to ask women to get involved at a leadership level is likely tied to the *impression* that they are not as engaged or willing as men. To address this impression, include training for the stakeholders in your organization charged with tracking and building lists of potential leaders. Most importantly, keep asking. As noted earlier, a "no" is not always forever. Moving from one phase of life to another may open up her capacity to serve.
- *Set a clear goal and path to grow the number of women leaders.* As described in Chapter 5, the College of William & Mary committed to have women fill 50 percent of volunteer leadership roles by 2020. Sue Warner, director of volunteer management at William & Mary, leads this charge. She believes that success likely will be due to both new

behaviors and math. The new behaviors include training, personal conversations, reporting on progress, nudging and constantly looking for more women to include in the pipeline. The math is the practical side—understanding terms, who is rolling off when and how many women need to be nominated and placed on the various boards to achieve the goal. The expectations for board leadership have not changed, but the approach and focus have.

- *Intentionally share expectations and the pathway to leadership.* At one university, I learned that a woman was a candidate to become a board trustee. A male trustee who thought highly of her sponsored her for the role. The university met with her twice and then offered her the position. It was only then that she learned the expectations, including the annual gift requirement. She let them know she could not meet that level and bowed out of the pool.

I've heard this story in many variations. Women in focus groups shared that they were never told they needed to give to serve on the board, and fundraisers lamented that there were no women in the pipeline giving at the board level. Assumptions are being made, and conversations are not happening.

Seeing a higher percentage of women on leadership groups certainly is an important visual for those considering this position. In addition, women sharing with each other their own path to leadership is critical. In one focus group, women shared the idea of women "tapping" each other to share their stories of leadership and how to be effective in that role.

Women are discerning and want to be smart in making their decisions. Current leadership nomination processes may leave out the needed time and space to ask questions about how one might balance work, home, and this volunteer role, or what is truly expected or how to have true impact. Peer conversations can more easily elicit this open exchange of concerns and information.

- *Create an advisory council to help increase the number of women leaders.* Many initiatives focused on women's support start with a task force or advisory council. This group may include both staff and current volunteer leaders, as well as other individuals who are willing to serve, care about the mission and will add value. Starting with this leadership group provides credibility and a wide variety of resources for the work ahead. In addition, it may be from this group that you develop a pipeline of new leaders that may move on to other leadership roles in your organization.

Every example and tip to involve women listed in this section—from short-shots to long-term community building and leadership opportunities—worked for the organization because of a few key components:

- *The strategies were not designed in a vacuum.* Women stakeholders were listened to and often part of the design. This step cannot be circumvented. It will take longer to "fix" the resulting issues of non-participation than to spend a few extra hours up front gaining women's input and buy-in. This is all about building relationships in the very best sense of our profession.
- *The strategies were personally meaningful.* Even if it was a short conversation or two with a faculty member, the interaction allowed the woman to connect to the mission. Participants felt they were making a difference with the time and resources they had available.
- *The strategies were authentic and often built on program assets already in place,* such as a homeless shelter's regular evening meal.

Often, though not always, involvement can deepen the woman's understanding of the organization and current initiatives and issues, as well as stir her imagination about what she might commit to with her resources. There is insightful information offered in a president's briefing or questions asked during a community service project. There is energy in connecting with a group focused on making a difference together. Relationships made during these efforts deepen and lengthen the time a woman might stay involved in your organization.

Metrics

Your metrics will tie to your chosen involvement activities. The metric examples below may help you decide what to measure and track:

- Establish the baseline for current engagement levels. Track over time the changes in *participation* rates.

- Using a survey, establish a baseline for current *perception* of engagement, including the value of engagement and the sense of being part of a community. Updated surveys can measure changes.
- Design a process to assess and track life stages.
- Design and track a process of engaging a woman's network.
- Create a baseline of the number of women in the pipeline for leadership positions, tracking the number of women who have moved into leadership roles each year and changes in the percentage of women in the pipeline.
- Design and track a process to tag women who are having high-impact involvement with your mission (or similar involvement elsewhere) who are not in the leadership pipeline.
- Design and track a process to have peer conversations about leadership engagement.

CHAPTER TAKE-AWAYS

There is a myth that involving women takes longer. The specific ideas in this chapter are presented to show it is just different—a different conversation about joining a board, a different way to track and recognize life changes, a different design for an event agenda so there is time for the community to share and bond. It only feels like it takes longer now because we may be using the wrong approach.

The key is respecting all that women have to offer. They have powerful resources that can help further your mission if they are recognized for more than what is in their purses.

As one woman said in a focus group, "This is not just about money. Women need to feel needed for something other than their money."

Design meaningful ways for women to be involved with your mission. Keep in mind that women (a) want to be heard and listened to, (b) often have important networks, (c) may want to collaborate and connect with others, (d) look for high-impact opportunities and (e) change their level of involvement to match the demands of different life phases.

Chapter 11

INVEST

"[The university] needs to be more aggressive when it comes to asking."
—Alumna, focus group quote

Overview

This chapter focuses on what women consider when making a philanthropic gift and is named out of deference to women who "invest" various resources to support the causes they care about. This chapter looks at one resource, money.

Remember that "women are nearly twice as likely as men to say that giving to charity is the most satisfying aspect of having wealth" (U.S. Trust 2013). According to research by the Women's Philanthropy Institute, women either drive or influence household giving. "Even if he's the one that made the money, she's going to be the real gatekeeper," Melinda Gates told the *New York Times* on July 21, 2013. "And she's got to go along with any philanthropic plan because it affects her and it affects their kids."

Women are increasingly making their own gifts at significant levels.

- The Madeira School, a Washington, D.C., independent boarding and day school for girls, announced in early 2016 that it had raised $46.2 million toward capital projects. Nine donors, all women, gave $1 million or more, and one alumna issued a $10 million challenge grant to kick

off the effort (https://grahampelton.com/the-madeira-school-press
-release-women-give-millions-to-support-all-girls-alma-mater).

- The College of William & Mary quietly kicked off its "Society of 1918,"
  a new women's giving initiative, in the fall of 2017. The university set a
  goal of raising $1 million in one year. It hoped that through personal
  conversations and a mailing to a small select group of women that it
  would find more than 100 donors willing to give at least $10,000 annu-
  ally to be part of this group and support a new alumnae fund. Within
  two months, the effort drew 107 members who gave $10,000 or more,
  and one who gave $100,000. The school's development staff saw potential
  and set a higher goal of $1,918,000 to grow the membership. Without
  further solicitation and still in less than one year they had 203 members
  and raised more than $1.5 million.
- Smith College completed a five-year, $486 million campaign in early
  2017. The campaign was the largest ever undertaken by a women's
  college. Female donors gave 93 gifts of $1 million or more, totaling
  60 percent of the total raised (https://www.smith.edu/news/smith
  -college-announces-successful-campaign).
- In early 2018, *The Economist* published an article on women who are
  wealthy, self-made billionaires. Their numbers have grown, and their
  giving has followed. Melissa Durda, director of the U.S.-based Syner-
  gos Institute's Global Philanthropists Circle, was quoted in the article
  saying that "independently wealthy women have gained confidence
  about giving," and are active in philanthropic circles where they learn
  from each other (*Economist* 2018).

Collaboration

Throughout this book, I've written about the power of the women's network,
and the desire to collaborate. This desire influences many, although not all,
women in their philanthropic decisions.

Across society, women network in many ways and philanthropy is no
exception. Women's philanthropic networks may be women pooling their
resources to create change in their communities, loose federations of women
working toward a common goal or women coming together under the
umbrella of a larger organization.

Giving circles are defined as groups of individuals who pool their resources
and decide together which organizations to support. A 2017 study of giving

circles found that women make up the majority of membership, and more than half of U.S. giving circles are women-only groups (Bearman et al. 2017, 5). An earlier study found that giving circles influence members to give more, and more strategically. These members also saw themselves as more highly engaged and more knowledgeable about philanthropy, nonprofits and the community through their participation in the collective giving groups (Eikenberry and Bearman 2009, 4).

Other circles are more of a community. Individual women make their gifts and through their commitments are part of a larger community of donors organizing around a common, specific intention. Members of Women Moving Millions do not give to the organization. They donate $1 million or more to their chosen causes that support women and girls. Yet they are members of WMM community. The WMM team designs annual summits, courses, conference calls and gatherings to enhance connections, learning about philanthropy and finance, sharing with each other and the building of a trusted community through shared experiences. Creating an intentional community supports the philanthropic path of current members and is attractive to many new members who are giving at this level for the first time.

The Maverick Collective is an initiative within a larger nonprofit organization, Population Services International. This collective has over 23 members giving at least $1 million over three years to improve the health of women and girls in developing countries. However, it is not only about charitable giving. These women also are engaged with their time, expertise and willingness to spend time in the countries and villages to learn about and help design solutions for the health issues women and girls face. This is an initiative intentionally designed by women, for women. The Maverick Collective knows that women want to be involved beyond their purse.

The United Way also has a way for women to bring all their assets together to support their communities. "Women United" is their women's leadership-council model. These councils are now in more than 165 local United Ways. In many councils, the minimum gift is $1,000 a year, although many stretch well beyond that. Since its inception in 2002, this group has collectively raised $1.5 billion with more than 70,000 involved women. These women also volunteer time and speak with a unified voice about changes needed in the community. In Milwaukee, the group set an audacious goal of reducing teen pregnancy by 46 percent in 10 years. They achieved a 50 percent reduction in seven years. This is the power of women coming together with all of their resources.

There are hundreds of examples of women's networks, giving circles and collaborative giving across our country in communities, universities, and nonprofits, as well as internationally. There is much to understand about the proliferation and variety of women's networks when we consider how a large number of women approach their philanthropy.

A key to understanding women's philanthropy is found in the *experiences* described by the women who join these circles or collectives. "I watch our members lifting each other up. They are not competing, they're supporting each other. Friendships are formed," said Kate Roberts, a co-founder of The Maverick Collective. "Many of our members have started collaborating under their own steam. They visit programs together or lend skills to each other's projects" (*Economist* 2018).

Women also connect on a personal level that is nurturing and supportive even when difficult decisions are being made. As Jessica Houssian, the former executive director of WMM, says, when women collaborate, they are not afraid to dig in and they often learn together as they work side by side on the complexities of the issue at hand.

Knowing that women interested in your mission may have a desire to give in concert with others and accelerate impact, how might you design intentional giving opportunities that are collective, not individual?

Family

Women consider multiple factors when they give, including their family. "I'm worried about how making this gift will affect my children," said one very wealthy donor in a University of San Francisco focus group. She was considering a significant gift and did not want her young children to gain a sense of entitlement by hearing about the amount. She later made another gift and designed how to involve her whole family.

This donor exemplifies a finding in the 2016 U.S. Trust Study of High Net Worth Philanthropy about the difference between men and women when asked about involving family. Almost 35 percent of the women surveyed wanted to involve children, grandchildren or other younger relatives in giving, versus 25 percent of men.

The Rockefeller Philanthropic Advisors have seen that while men may choose to make a gift without consulting with the family, women more often express an interest in involving the next generation. In the organization's guide on women and philanthropy, it notes that women donors might find themselves asking these questions:

- To what extent should I make decisions independently and to what extent should I consult family members in the next generation or generations?
- How do I balance the next generation's priorities with what I see as immediate philanthropic opportunities?
- How can I integrate our family's diverse philanthropic viewpoints and interests while keeping our giving enjoyable and rewarding? (*Rockefeller Philanthropy Advisors* 2017, 5)

Recognizing that women may consider more than themselves in the gift decision, do you ask about a woman's family considerations when she is discussing a potential gift?

Decision-Making

Previous chapters already have noted that women consider many more factors than men when making a purchase decision. The same is true in how they invest their money.

The U.S. Trust 2014 Report on Women and Wealth notes that there is a measurable difference in how men and women approach risk, with women being more risk-averse (U.S. Trust 2014, 4). Wells Fargo found that "women and men may have a different mindset. In our survey, women tended to invest more conservatively than men" (Wells Fargo 2017, 3).

The Boston Consulting Group added more nuance on how women approach investing. In their 2010 report, *Leveling the Playing Field*, they offer the following:

> Women often focus on long-term investment goals and seek holistic advice. Women tend to set clear goals—usually in response to, or in anticipation of, life changes—and they want their investment strategy, and its ongoing execution, to revolve around these objectives. Women are more intent on understanding the risk-return profiles of investments as they relate to their overarching goals and financial security. (Damisch 2010, 6)

This intentional investment alignment with life goals and phases is understandable. Women's approach to their money is born out of the reality of their lives. They know their earnings may increase and decrease over their lifetimes as they make career adjustments based on life changes such as child birth and aging parents. They pay attention to their retirement savings knowing they will live longer.

I believe that saying that women are risk-averse when they invest may be an over-simplification. Based on personal experience and the research, I believe that women are discerning and thoughtful and that they anchor their investment decisions in complex goals. Research shows that women consider multiple factors in purchases, and so the same behavior may spill over into a woman's philanthropy. The WPI 2018 report, *Giving by and for Women*, was based on qualitative interviews with 23 high-net-worth women who had made a gift or commitment of $1 million or more. The study finds that these women believe it is critical to educate themselves before making funding decisions. They research, talk to other women donors and take time to absorb, probe and learn.

Many nonprofits talk about the time it takes for a woman to decide to make a gift.

> For many women, philanthropy is less about recognition and visibility, and more about building relationships, achieving a deep understanding of what their gift will do, and the impact the journey has on their life. In my experience, women often need more time to write a check. They want time to understand the problem, the intervention, and their role in the solution. But once they make a commitment, they're likely to invest for the long term. Be patient. (Houssian 2016)

If you believe that a woman may be in a learning process, how might you set up philanthropic conversations differently? What might be possible if you considered yourself an advisor, rather than a fundraiser, as you build a relationship with her?

Asking

Perhaps because we have not focused on women, or we subscribe to the misconception that they are risk-averse, or believe that they take too long to decide or we lack a clear view of their full giving capacity because they give across many organizations—or because of dozens of other myths mentioned in this book—we are not asking enough women for significant gifts. One woman donor I interviewed said:

> I know I'm one of the largest donors to this organization. But they still aren't asking me for enough. They don't know my capacity, and they don't know how to ask me. They are great leaders, but they are missing a big opportunity.

In one focus group for a university's women donors, I heard:

I'm an alumna with the means to make a gift who is starving for contact.

If someone doesn't ask, we don't give. I'm fine being asked for more than my capacity, being asked by a close relationship that I trust, and have the ask tailored to what I care about.

In a 2011 study, researchers at Indiana University asked women and men why they stopped supporting an organization. While 61.2 percent of men said they were over-solicited or asked for an inappropriate amount, only 49.3 percent of women said the same. The research is telling us that women are less likely to feel over-solicited, an important finding for you and your team as you build your women's philanthropy strategies (Center on Philanthropy 2011).

Previous chapters talk about adaptations to identify and research women and involve them. Yes, the adaptations provide a strong foundation for building a relationship and helping her see how she can have impact. Asking is part of relationship building. We can get caught in an engagement swirl, or in the myths. We can get so close to the women through cultivation that we assume they will see the need and step up. However, we can't assume. As the quotes above indicate, a woman deserves the courtesy of an ask that is significant and will have the impact she desires.

How might you adapt your strategies knowing that many (although not all) women are willing to consider a significant ask? Reflect on yourself as well. What might be holding you back from making a bolder request?

Desired Outcome

It is important to address where women want to make an impact. Many believe that women prefer to give to women and girls. If there is a scholarship fund, they'll want it for female students. If it is a science initiative, they'll want to boost the number of female scientists.

But is this perception true? The answer is "sometimes." We know that women certainly support non-gender-specific causes across the majority of charitable subsectors they support (see Chapter 1). In a 2016 study, WPI found that more than 46 percent of women donated to at least one cause aimed at women and girls, compared with 37 percent of men. Women are more likely than men to give to women's and girls' causes, but they do not do so universally (Mesch et al. 2016).

In giving across most charitable subsectors, some women (and some men) will give to women's and girls' causes at certain times for certain reasons. We cannot assume without asking. Women will tell you what they care about, and why. And what they care about can shift over time according to life stages, income and current goals. As we present opportunities to our women prospects, it is up to us to tailor them in powerful ways to show impact according to how she wants to make a difference in the world. As one University of San Francisco alumna said in a focus group:

> How is USF contributing to the world? Tell me that story—about how we are really changing the world. I know the mission statement but give me specifics. Tell me the positive impact we are having, on what, on whom and why it is so important. Now *that* is enticing.

How might you ask, rather than assume, what a woman wants to give to? How might you present a provocative and bold opportunity for her to make a significant difference?

Design

What can you do to create a community of women supporting you at significant levels? The act of asking for a gift is very individual and depends on the woman's personal concerns and your relationship with her. The solicitation for every woman will be different, just as it is for men. Yet, as noted above, there are gender differences when women consider making the gift. Therefore, the design examples below are chosen to help you address those considerations and build the right conversations and environment in which there is a higher likelihood that more women will give significantly to your organization.

Start with Curiosity

Knowing all the considerations a woman *might* have, what questions could you ask her? Imagine if the first conversation included little or nothing about the organization and instead you just tried to learn more about her thoughts and interests. Beth Mann of the Jewish Federations of North America uses this strategy. She shared with me:

> I find it is important to truly have a conversation, maybe even a second one, before making an ask. I make her the reason for the encounter and not the gift. It is my time to learn about her and understand what she cares about.

In just about every scenario, this mindset of learning first leads to a gift that is not only a quality gift but one that is repeated and increased each year as the relationship to the organization and its mission grows.

In the Appreciative Inquiry model, discovery is the first step. What if we used the first conversation or two with a woman to discover? Discovery is not just about learning. It allows for relationship building, appreciation of values, and creating a common understanding from which to move forward. Open-ended, curious questions that allow for reflection help our donors connect to purpose in their increasingly fast, transactional lives.

Imagine asking her:

- What has been your most fulfilling philanthropic experience? Can you recall a time that is memorable and really stands out, a time when you felt most alive, effective and excited about your involvement?
  - Share the details. What made it an exciting experience?
  - Who else was involved?
  - What values did the experience draw upon?
- What do you want to preserve and/or promote? What matters deeply to you?
- What institutions are important to you in your life? Say more about why that is so.
- Where does our organization fall in your list of priorities? Say more about why.
  - This latter question is not obnoxious if asked with genuine curiosity. It is very helpful to learn more about her values *and* priorities.

You will learn so much more from her story and the questions above than you can ever find in research or in a briefing. You will also open the possibility for a warm, growing relationship. Trust is built when people really feel they are heard.

During one training on asking open questions, a male participant spoke up and said that these types of questions don't work for men. He said men get right to the point and want to know what is needed. He is right; men are different from women. However, both genders appreciate being asked open-ended questions that allow them to consider core values and what they really care about. Charles Collier, former senior philanthropic advisor at Harvard University, wrote about this in his book, *Wealth in Families*. Ronald Schiller (2013, 2016) has written several books on partnerships with donors. He notes consistently that few fundraisers take the time to ask donors simple questions to learn what they want to accomplish with their philanthropy. How you ask these questions, and the number of questions you ask, may differ with women and men donors, but do consider asking. Virginia Gilbert Loftin, vice president for advancement at Birmingham-Southern College, shared:

> I am always looking for their story to learn what they deeply care about. I often will start with a question to hear their story. Men will share—they just frame it differently. When I was working at the University of Alabama at Birmingham, I met with a graduate of our optometry school who had made a recent gift to the school. When I asked him why he chose optometry, he said, "I was a preacher's kid, and when I was in fifth grade, I was the shortest kid in the class, played the clarinet and wore Coke-bottle glasses. A really geeky kid. But the year I turned 15, I grew nine inches, and I got contacts—and those contacts changed my life. I gave up the clarinet, took up sports and had a lot more success with girls. So, I knew I wanted to change the lives of other geeky kids."
>
> I was touched by his story and could tell he was touched as well when he retold it. As I was leaving, he asked: "If I wanted to do something more, could I?" And he did—he made another gift soon after our visit.

Cultivate with Curiosity

Additional questions are valuable throughout the cultivation and solicitation process. In subsequent conversations, it is helpful to ask her:

- How are charitable decisions made in the home?
- Does she want to make a gift on her own or with her spouse and/or family?
  - If she wants to include others in the family, how does she suggest you build those relationships—with individual meetings, or with her?
- Does she want to be part of a collaborative giving effort?
  - What questions does she have about making a gift?

Such straightforward questions will strengthen the relationship and continue to build trust. Women appreciate probing questions from their investment advisors. It is powerful if you position yourself as a partner who is willing to listen and provide options to help her achieve her goals.

Sheree Meredith, vice president for philanthropic services at the Hamilton Community Foundation in Canada, considers herself a partner with her prospective donors. She shared a story of a member of Women 4 Change who wanted to give more to the initiatives-grants fund. Meredith listened to her, acknowledged the option, but then asked where the woman wanted to have a big impact. Through Meredith's questions, the donor got in touch with her commitment to education and ended up co-founding, with Hamilton Community Foundation, a significant, 10-year education effort in the community. The donor continues to support the Women 4 Change grants in addition to becoming a change-agent on an issue close to her heart.

Curiosity goes both ways. Women will ask in-depth questions of you as they consider their potential gift. Consider her questions as due diligence and listen to them with curiosity, not defensiveness. She may be inquiring about the problem you are trying to solve to determine what role she might play. Take time to listen and learn what is prompting her questions. Your responding in turn with good follow-up questions will help you respond to her true concerns, versus just answering her question.

Your prospect may also be curious about how to make her gift. As fundraisers, we know to deepen the relationship by connecting her with other organizational leaders and staff to answer her questions and share more about the need. A way to enhance this best practice is to ask a current donor to share her philanthropic journey and how she made a large gift. We have many visible examples in print or in storytelling of how men make large gifts but far fewer about how women make these decisions. Peer conversations on this topic can be powerful, and many questions can be answered in a personal setting.

The world of business has intentionally created a new form of mentoring for women—sponsorship to help talented women navigate their careers and be visible to leaders. Nonprofits can adapt this approach to connect women to peers that can help them navigate their philanthropic journey. Some organizations design donor-education forums. Others set up individual meetings between current donors and prospects. Connecting her to others is another way to perform your role as trusted partner.

The cultivation process is also the time to help bring out her "dream." The questions above will cause her to reflect on the facts of giving. But what about the impact she wants to make in the world? What is she hoping to accomplish with the gift? What is the larger purpose she cares about? What does she long to change for her children and the next generation? What could catalyze her to an even more significant gift for her desired impact? This last question is not a set up to push for more money. Rather, you are investigating to learn what barriers she is concerned about and help her imagine even larger possibilities.

You learned about her values in the initial conversations. These later questions help her reflect on how she wants to build those values into her philanthropy and create her own vision to make an impact on something larger than her own life. Staying curious will help you provide time and space so she can share her thought process and the considerations that she is weighing to achieve her goals.

Make Philanthropy Overt

Before we look at how you ask, I want to underscore one point made in Chapter 4. All throughout the relationship with a woman, the need for philanthropic support must be overt. While *leading* with philanthropy may not work, given women's desire to be involved and discerning, the conversation about providing financial support when the time is right should not be ignored. One unspoken belief of many of the women's philanthropy programs in the past 25 years was "build it and they will come *and* give." As discussed earlier, there were many reasons that didn't happen. One cannot assume that a woman's engagement will lead to her philanthropic support for you.

Duke University knew about this disconnect when it designed its women's philanthropy approach in 2013. When it created a task force of women donors and leaders, it was clear about the compelling need to grow women's financial support. At first, many task-force members wanted an inclusive program for all Duke women to be engaged and focus on gifts of all sizes. As the committee members slowly learned about all the ways that women were already engaged with and giving to Duke, they began to focus on the major-gift gap. Duke alumnae were not making major gifts in amounts and frequency equal to men. The participants, on their own, chose to prioritize solving this issue. They created their vision and then designed around the clear intent.

If the Duke staff had not stayed anchored in the university's philanthropic vision, the task force may have recommended an engagement model that did not lead to significant philanthropy. Instead, Duke is gaining the philanthropy *and* leadership of women who are joining the recently designed Women's Impact Network. Individuals become members when they cross the threshold of $100,000 in cumulative lifetime giving. Recently, the network introduced lower tiered membership thresholds for younger undergraduate alumnae to encourage them to establish a pattern of giving back to Duke and strengthen the pipeline for volunteer leaders and donors.

Make Powerful Asks

A key design element for a powerful ask is: Just do it!

We hold ourselves back. A colleague shared that when she recently was considering a donation request of a woman supporter, she did start with a high number. But then she worried about offending the prospect. She knew how much the family paid in school tuition and recognized the woman had spent many hours working on a recent gala. So, the fundraiser talked herself down to a lower request.

One of my favorite quotes came from a group of women leaders talking about being bold in their giving. One woman said: "We won't jump over a chasm in two steps."

We do have a chasm in women's giving, caused by myths and inattention. It is time to jump. When we make a few bold asks, the rest become easier. In 2014, the vice principal of university advancement at McGill University was curious about the potential of women's philanthropy and asked his team to review research and design a few ideas. Even before that work had been completed, he boldly asked for, and received, a $1 million gift from an alumna who had not given even close to that level before. He became convinced about the untapped potential of women alumnae. His leadership helped McGill to adjust behaviors and analytics to grow the pipeline of women donors.

My design challenge to you is **ask a woman for the boldest amount you believe is possible.** Don't second-guess yourself. When you ask boldly and provide compelling details of the potential impact, important and authentic conversations about possibility and change will happen, rather than smaller logistical conversations about making the gift.

Consider Collaborative Giving Opportunities

A best practice to achieve a funding goal is to create a pyramid of donors. Who are the few within our donor pipeline who can give the most? These top prospects are asked for large leadership gifts that help meet the bulk of the goal. Many other donors join at lower levels.

What if there was another lens through which to consider women's support? If you want an image, consider a lively, green hill populated at the top with many major donors. When you ask many to give at a significant level, such as Women Moving Millions asking for $1 million gifts, or Duke setting a cumulative lifetime giving threshold of $100,000, you can grow women's philanthropy at an accelerated pace. And the women on the hilltop find community, which builds sustainability for your organization. Why wouldn't you design collaborative giving opportunities?

Dartmouth College created this design.

In early 2014, a small group of dedicated alumnae set an ambitious goal to recruit 100 Dartmouth women to make gifts of $100,000 or more to honor the 100th anniversary of the Dartmouth College Fund. The response was extraordinary: in less than three months, 114 women joined the Centennial Circle and raised almost $15 million to support current students through financial aid—demonstrating the strength of community and the commitment shared by the women of Dartmouth. The Circle currently has 175 members and is open to all Dartmouth alumnae. (http://www.dartmouth centennialcircle.com/about/)

How did Dartmouth women achieve this remarkable outcome? Dartmouth already had a successful annual giving program—the second largest in the country. Catherine Craighead Briggs, a graduate of the Class of 1988 at Dartmouth, had already been a leader for her class's 25th reunion campaign. When she learned about the 100th anniversary, she wanted to spearhead a bold effort of women soliciting women to give $100,000 each to the Dartmouth College Fund. Catherine shared the following at the 2017 Chronicle of Philanthropy Symposium:

Women are different. We are relational, not hierarchical. We want to belong to something with meaning. And we will hold collective responsibility. I thought if we set a big audacious goal, and raised money for financial aid for women, we'd help level the playing field.

I also know that women don't lead alone. I identified two co-chairs, and a group of leaders to design the effort. We were all involved in the planning, together with the staff. We knew we wanted to leverage our networks, so we designed peer conversations and solicitations. We were about more than asking for a gift—we wanted to cultivate a community. And we knew this community would want to do more than just give, so we designed ways for them to know the impact of their gifts, get involved, and received intellectual stimulation from the university and our gatherings.

When we began asking, we made sure it was a peer asking, someone they connected with. Sometimes two or three conversations were needed to answer questions and show impact. We hoped for 50 members in three months and got 114. Women from all ages gave, and many who had never given before gave at that level.

Mindi Laine, director of the Dartmouth Centennial Circle, also shared with me:

We are now five years into the Centennial Circle and see great power in the notion that the Circle never closes. We have 175 members, and current members continue to give leadership gifts annually. I believe this is replicable if you have strong volunteers to lead the effort, an inspiring vision and dedicated staff support. The peer-to-peer solicitations—and ability to share the vision—were key to our success.

It was important to have a big goal with a big impact (financial aid in this case). It caught women's imaginations and brought them forward to be part of this exciting initiative. Being part of the community keeps them engaged and inspired to continue to give back to Dartmouth.

We've seen a lasting halo effect of the Centennial Circle. In 2012, women giving $10,000 gifts only made up 18 percent of the annual fund. In 2016, they were 29 percent. In the same time frame, the percent of women giving $30,000 gifts grew from 27 percent to 50 percent and giving $100,000 annually grew from 4 percent to 20 percent. The Centennial Circle women have forged a new path for philanthropy at Dartmouth. Every year, they continue to generously support Dartmouth while also inspiring other women to increase their giving at every level.

Dartmouth President Phil Hanlon also praised the Centennial Circle program for its effectiveness in growing women's giving for the school at every level:

Without question, alumnae in the Circle are trailblazers, and they're taking philanthropy in a new, deeply meaningful direction. Women accounted for 31 percent of total giving to the Dartmouth College Fund during the past year, up from 22 percent five years ago, and Dartmouth alumnae are closing the gender giving gap at all levels. I believe the Circle is driving this change, and in the coming years, I expect even more alumnae will follow the Circle's lead and invest in the future of our students.

Dartmouth's program looks like a sustainable green hilltop to me. Consider how you might design a similar effort to support your organization.

Metrics

Depending on what you design, build metrics to track progress and ensure accountability. Refer to this list to see which ones match your design or stimulate your thinking of others that might serve.

- Basic data metrics
  - Overall giving by women
  - Increase in number of women giving
  - Percentage of women making increased gifts
  - Percentage of women in your donor portfolios, and the change in that percentage
  - Percentage of women asked, and the change in that percentage

- Advanced metrics
  - Knowledge of decision-making in the household
  - Percentage of women making their largest gift to your organization
  - Number of bold funding opportunities that resonate with women
  - Number of collaborative funding opportunities to present to women
  - If you design a women's collaborative-giving initiative, also measure the halo effect on all women's giving.

CHAPTER TAKE-AWAYS

Women prefer to be heard and known before being asked.
- Take time to ask about her values and goals.
- Learn about her vision and what she wants to accomplish.

Women hold multiple considerations in mind when making a gift decision.
- Be curious in your cultivation.
- Provide time and space for her questions.

Women may choose to collaborate with others to amplify giving.
- Create collaborative giving opportunities.

Women do give, and want their gifts to have meaningful impact.
- Present the ask as an opportunity to achieve her vision.
- Consider peer solicitation.
- Be bold when you ask.

Chapter 12

IMPACT

*"Donors are partners, not targets. Tell me the impact
of what we are doing together."*
—Interview with alumna

Overview

This chapter is called "Impact" because that is what great stewardship is all about—helping each donor understand the impact of her or his gift.

Stewardship is simply a part of building and further cementing the donor relationship. Stewardship builds trust, a core of the relationship with any donor and particularly women. (Can I trust you to do what you said you would do with my money?) Trust is personal and grown one action at a time. Impact is a natural extension of trust. Impact is about social responsibility. One's concern about and interest in social responsibility flows from trust in the organization.

Most donors expect trust and look for the impact, but women do so more often.

The Lilly Family School of Philanthropy at Indiana University looked at gender differences in the expectations donors held of nonprofits when they made a gift and reported that 45.3 percent of women and 26.4 percent of men wanted communication about the impact of the gift (Center on Philanthropy 2011). In the same study, women expected more ongoing communication than men (45 percent vs. 36 percent), expected that the organization would honor their requests for how the gift was to be used (80.4 percent vs. 68.4 percent) and expected they would be offered involvement with the organization (15 percent vs. 5.3 percent). These were all statistically significant differences.

Virginia Gilbert Loftin of Birmingham-Southern College shared with me: "All donors want to know about impact. It is no longer true—if it ever was true—that men are transactional and women are relational. We should be appealing to men's hearts too. Having an emotional connection is equally important for men and women. They just express it differently."

The difference can show up in the questions asked up front to discern the likely impact. The example below shows how women focus with greater depth on the impact to the beneficiaries before they decide on the gift.

When the board of the $100 million Plough Foundation in Memphis was debating whether to finance a family safety center for victims of domestic violence, the six male trustees asked the applicants for "a complete breakdown of the population and how it's changed over the years by area," recalled Diane Rudner, the board chairwoman. By contrast, the four women wanted to know "how it affected the children, where they go to school, and how to keep the families together." Ultimately, the foundation gave the center $1 million in 2010. (Hawthorne 2012)

With this level of attention on the potential impact to the beneficiaries before a gift is made, one can assume that the same desire to learn about the impact in detail is important to women after the gift is made. From various alumnae at the College of William & Mary focus groups:

- For me, the catalyst to give more was seeing the impact. Seeing people passionate about what they're doing and receiving information about how many lives are impacted by the organization—that's driven my involvement.
- When you hear from the people your gift is helping, that's particularly moving. I have an interest in the cause and want to see how the money is used. That makes me want to give more. I'm a financial person by background but I connect emotionally about my impact.
- I look for stories on the individuals benefitting. I love getting letters from the students; they tell me what they did over the summer with our research grant.

- I want to see the outcomes from my contributions. Will the money make a difference? How does it translate?
- Seeing results is so important. This is what really increased our amount of giving to [another organization].

These women shared that emotional connection to impact was the primary motivation for giving and giving again, to William & Mary and other causes. The interviewees wanted their money to make a difference or solve a problem. They wanted details about the impact (facts), and also to see and be connected with the results (stories, witnessing the mission in action).

Before moving to Birmingham-Southern College to lead advancement, Virginia Gilbert Loftin was the assistant vice president for development communications and principal gifts at the University of Alabama at Birmingham. She shared that she was adamant that communications and stewardship were not about giving numbers or dollar figures—it was about connecting money to mission. She learned this in her first job as a volunteer fundraiser at Birmingham's Young Women's Christian Association:

> We were raising funds for a daycare center for homeless children, and I learned that speaking about the children's needs brought in more and larger gifts. We let donors know that children in this special program took more naps than in a conventional setting because shelters can be noisy places, and because uncertainty is often exhausting for little folks. They also ate more, because even at a tender age, they had somehow sensed they might not be able to count on their next meal. Our fundraising case was to ensure that each child had a place to rest, plenty to eat and a cubby with his or her name on it—a place that was their own. That was a more powerful message than the program costs and budget gaps. And with this focus, we were able to continue to share the impact this safe place had on those children and on their mothers.

How women desire to learn about impact before giving carries over to how best to steward them. Their behaviors don't stop at the gift. They expect to hear specifics on how they are part of making a difference. They will ask questions about what is working and what is not. Many will stay involved and be part of the next iteration of what might be tried. Many women will also share stories of the impact with others and why they are excited to be part of the mission.

At the 2017 Women's Philanthropy Institute Symposium, a panel on how women invest in their philanthropy coined a phrase: "Women give their time, talent, treasure *and testimony.*" As Witter and Chen shared in *The She Spot*, women are natural marketers. They wrote: "For nonprofits . . . seeking to gain support, women who are true believers can help make believers of others by spreading the good word to friends and family or by simply giving their honest appraisal of why they're . . . supporting an issue" (Witter and Chen 2008, 16). Testimony is an important outcome when you steward women well. When you build their trust, answer their questions and demonstrate impact through stories as well as facts, you may well connect to more women who might support you.

Design

This section is not about lots of stewardship ideas. There are plenty of those in our fundraising best practices, and I know that your stewardship activities are best tied to the culture of your organization. This section provides ideas to help increase the ways you communicate impact and help women share that information with others. If we remember that the way we connect to women has a high likelihood of also connecting to other women, men and the next generation, enhancing stewardship programs in ways that resonate with women is just good business.

Keep Building the Relationship

A speaker at an annual gathering for the National Panhellenic Conference Foundations Leadership Summit asked the audience: "What are we doing to make a difference in a donor's life, versus talk about what a donor is doing for an organization?" Sharing impact is one way to make a difference in a woman donor's life. To do this, you can:

Maintain your curiosity

Your relationship is built on connection, and you grow that connection each time you are open and curious, rather than transactional. At every turn in the relationship, including stewardship, ask her questions such as:

- How are you feeling about your gift?
- What do you hope for the future (of the project) (of the organization)?
- What more would you like to learn about?

Answer her questions

Just as a woman asks more questions before making a gift, there may be questions that arise as her gift is put to use (according to her instructions). Take the time to listen and provide answers. This may require bringing others into the conversation to help provide the information.

I was stewarding a woman donor for the American Red Cross many years ago. The gift had gone to a Russian orphanage, run by the Red Cross of that region. The donor asked many, many questions and we needed to get information from our finance team, our own international program team and the Red Cross in that Russian region. While it took time to answer all the questions, the fact that we did led to a significantly larger second gift for similar needs.

Keep recognizing her value

Every donor deserves to be treated well, listened to and valued. As noted in Chapter 9 on inspiring communication, women expect connection and can be sensitive to their sense of inclusion in your organization.

What does that look like? Women will let you know the level of communication and engagement they are looking for after they give—just ask. From a focus group:

- "The organization did a good job making a connection with me, but once I made my gift, there was little communication after."
- "I'm getting emails from [the leader] after I made my gift. The organization kept the communication going. I love hearing when big things happen. And I like being listened to."
- "I like being invited to the organizational events. I often can't make it, but just being invited makes a difference."

Increase Your Stewardship

It may be obvious from the points above, but pay attention to the number of stewardship touch points (visits, calls, emails) with women. Per the WPI research, it is unlikely that women will feel they are getting too much communication. Having more than one touch point to thank her for a gift allows you to ask questions, check in, share the impact and show that she is valued.

Give Recognition per Her Wishes

You cannot assume women do or do not want to be publicly recognized after making their gifts. There is a myth that women don't want recognition and that they prefer to make anonymous gifts. That is no longer true. Many women are making significant gifts and choosing to be public about them. At the same time, it is also true that recognition is not important for many women donors.

The 2018 WPI report *Giving by and for Women* addressed recognition in interviews with the participants. Here's what one woman, Alice, shared:

> There's women [who] want their name on everything, that's reality. But I think more of us just want to see the change bad enough. That it's not so much about building your ego. I don't see my ego in philanthropy at all. I see my heart. If no one names anything after me, I'll be very happy. I just think that's kind of useless, to put my name on a building. But I'm actually less the kind of person who wants to receive an award and more the kind of person who would like to see the work that I have done and the money I have given help people—and they get up and talk about the difference it made. That means so much more to me. (O'Connor et al. 2018, 28)

Another woman in the same study changed her stance on recognition after learning it could extend her impact:

> [I] didn't want to go public on it. We went and had a whole thing about that, but then they told me there was somebody younger than me who wanted to give a million-dollar gift, so I should announce it so that she would feel comfortable giving. (Ibid, 29)

Help Her Learn Through Experience

We understand impact more quickly and directly when we can experience it. This is one reason both The Maverick Collective and the Jewish Federations design field experiences for their members. Putting women donors on the ground to witness the programs they are supporting was powerful and, in both cases, led to sustained support at many levels, including funding, time and expertise.

Not every organization can take the donor directly "into the field." How do you bring the mission to the donor? Universities have students write personal letters of gratitude, noting what is now possible in their lives. The American Red Cross staff have sent donors smartphone pictures, in real time, of the devastation the disaster created, with a personal note thanking them for their gift. During annual events, nonprofits ask their beneficiaries to share their personal story of overcoming hardship during annual events. One nonprofit helping the homeless invites donors in to make peanut butter and jelly sandwiches that the staff will deliver that night. During these food-prep sessions, they hear about the organization's services and impact.

All of these interactions intimately connect the donor to what her gift is supporting. These experiences are personal and have emotional resonance. They connect to the heart, as well as the mind. You are helping her investment come to life when she sees the impact first hand or through an eye-opening photo, personal letter or compelling story.

Share Stories as Well as Statistics

Stories can be powerful to describe impact. Virginia Gilbert Loftin shared with me:

> Dollar figures are not interesting—who gave how much for what. In fact, focusing on gift amounts can be a limiting factor for readers. Someone reading about a $2 million gift may think, "I can't give at that level, so my gift won't matter," and another person with capacity to give even more may think, "They only need $2 million." So I push to focus on impact. What was made possible because of that gift? How? I want our stories to connect to the donor's story of how and why she made the gift, not the amount given. I believe impact stories create personal connections for the donor we are writing about, and all the readers who might provide support.

Sometimes fundraisers can feel removed from the mission. It can be hard for us to be in the field or in a classroom as we frenetically juggle all the demands of our profession. Others may feel that the organization doesn't easily show impact; its mission is research or providing umbrella support and training for its member nonprofits working on the ground. That is why we may "report" on the facts of the mission, rather than share our own experiences about the mission. We miss out on an opportunity to deepen personal connections when we are just reporting.

I spoke with Maggie Steig, a leadership coach, actor and story teller. She trained me and my husband on how to tell compelling stories. Maggie recognizes the difficulty of telling a story of impact that was not experienced first-hand, yet she shared some helpful points:

- When you are telling a story, you are the one connecting to the audience. It is through you that they can connect to the mission, so they first need to feel a connection to you.
    - You need to be willing and open to your own feelings and emotions about the mission and its impact.
    - Get as many personal touch points with the impact as possible. Look at photos, read letters from beneficiaries and listen to their stories, interview the program people and feel what they are describing. This is about you feeling the mission, not just listing all the accomplishments.
- Use present tense and bring the donor into the experience. Maggie used this example:
    - "I'm sitting at my desk five months after the project started. It is a gray day and I'm feeling heavy with all the to-dos for the day. The phone rings from the project leader in the field, and she begins to share an extraordinary story of a family in that town that just . . . I couldn't wait to tell you the story."
- Be congruent. This is about alignment of your mood, tone, emotion, body and words. In the story above, you would be expressing excitement at what you heard through all these modalities.
- Think about talking in broad brush strokes to paint a picture, rather than reporting. People can get lost in words and try to speak the written word. That can feel long. Keep it simple, short and connected to emotions.
    - Rehearse. She shared the Mark Twain quote: "It takes three weeks of rehearsal to be spontaneous." While you may not need weeks of rehearsal, you also don't want to tell a story without practicing it. Tell it to a few people and get feedback.

I believe that powerful storytelling about impact is critical for women and will also help with other donors in your portfolio. You do have many emotionally connecting stories you can tell about the impact of your organization, and I encourage you to learn how to tell them. As one speaker implored fundraisers at a panel on media and storytelling during the 2017 WPI Symposium, "Be the strongest, clearest, most passionate voice you can be."

Connect to the Community

Given that many women prefer to collaborate when they give, and/or become part of a giving community, there is a design opportunity to show impact to the group as well as an individual.

- One early funding opportunity for members of the President's Council of Cornell Women was to provide seed grants to women faculty doing early research that was not ready for big grants. During membership events, the women faculty who received these grants were invited to meet the members and discuss their research.
- A group of women donors to a sorority foundation were invited to be part of a leadership training for young sorority leaders about to graduate. The donors not only saw the use of curriculum they had supported, but also gained personal stories from today's women on campus.
- The National Women's History Museum invites donors and guests to participate in regular group calls to hear from the board chair about the latest legislative activities to build the museum in Washington, as well as the growth of communities of support for this effort around the country.

When a group of women learns about impact at the same time, there is a bond and common understanding that is shared. They think, "We are making this difference together. What else might we do together?" The sense of being part of something bigger can be exponentially amplified as each person turns to others in the community to share her feelings about the impact and desires for the future.

Spread Testimonials

In addition to sharing within a community, many women may also tell their network about their experiences and the impact. This will grow your visibility at a minimum and also may grow your pipeline. You can design ways to capitalize on women's willingness to talk to family and friends about their involvement and the changes they are part of.

A leader of the United Way of Greater Milwaukee and Waukesha County spoke at the Philanthropy NEXT summit held by the *Chronicle of Philanthropy*. She noted that the Women United Network of their United Way were donors *and* actors to help significantly reduce teen pregnancy in less than five years. They not only gave their own financial support but also spread the word as results were released each year. They shared the stories they heard, forwarded videos that were created, brought their friends and family to events and proudly spread the fact that there was a drop in the number of teen pregnancies each year.

This example used program materials and events that were already created for the initiative to help the women share their enthusiasm and commitment. What could you re-purpose to help women talk about your impact with others?

Metrics

Sharing compelling impact often leads to strengthened relationships and increases the probability of more support (time, talent, treasure and testimony). Design metrics that measure the robustness of your stewardship efforts:

- Create a baseline and track any changes in the number of stewardship touch points with women.
- Train, and then track the number of organizational staff who tell compelling stories of impact. Set a goal to increase this number over time.
- Design a qualitative survey about what is resonating about your impact and track this over time.
- Track the difference between sharing impact with the woman donor individually, or with her group, and any difference in her subsequent growth in giving and overall support.
- Track the frequency of your women donors sharing your impact with their networks.

You are looking for the ripple effect of quality interactions—between your impact (measures and stories) and the donor or group of donors, between donors themselves and between donors and their networks. You also want to learn about and track what happens after those interactions. How does the donor's relationship with you change? The idea is that the repercussions of sharing compelling impact are bigger than they seem. How might it deepen relationships, broaden your donor base and increase funding? I encourage you to have a curious mindset about the power of sharing impact and the many benefits across time that it can bring to your women donors, to your organization and to your larger community.

CHAPTER TAKE-AWAYS

Women look for impact before making a gift and expect to hear about the impact afterward.

- Anticipate her questions on impact, take time to answer them and build a deeper relationship.

Women want to be emotionally connected to a gift's impact and beneficiaries, in addition to hearing the facts.

- Help women experience the impact themselves, if possible.
- Create and share your own personal and compelling stories about impact.
- Share information in groups to amplify the sense of impact and excitement for what more might be done.

Women are natural marketers and will share your impact with their networks.

- Provide her with materials and highlights to share proudly with family and friends.
- Letting her know in multiple ways the impact she is creating for the beneficiaries can build a longer and stronger relationship that may lead to deeper support on many levels.

Part IV

DESTINY

Chapter 13

THE SUSTAINING POWER
OF A TEAM APPROACH

"Destiny is not a matter of chance; it is a matter of choice.
It is not a thing to be waited for, it is a thing to be achieved."
—William Jennings Bryan

Overview

Organizations are perfectly designed to get the results they get. With current organizational designs, we've been limited in accelerating women's giving. It is not sufficient to "know" about the research on how women give and ask a staff member to spearhead a program for women. Sustained giving and support from women needs our collective awareness, leadership, creativity, innovation and team cooperation and it requires organizational change.

One of the reasons I chose the Appreciative Inquiry framework for this book is because it opens individual and organizational power and creativity in a generative way. Using Appreciative Inquiry can lead to previously unimagined cooperation and commitment, and from that comes innovative new actions based on a compelling vision held by many. I believe this framework produces the behavioral and organizational changes needed in our sector to accelerate women's philanthropy.

By now, if you've been following the recommendations, you have significantly more than one staff member invested in women's philanthropy. You have engaged a team of stakeholders, from leaders to staff to volunteers, as well as donors who have told their stories to your organizational team. You shifted involvement from a few to many. Together you understand your uniqueness, the research on how women give and the unconscious myths that may have been barriers. There is group support around a compelling vision and your specific intentions. You've reviewed your own discovery inputs, plus the many examples in this book, and designed your actions to align with your vision and intentions.

The energy, momentum and practical design you've created is what will carry you into your destiny, which is integrating women throughout your fundraising. This last step is also known as "delivery," comprised of the timelines, action steps and accountabilities. Certainly, all those are needed to achieve your goals. However, this final step would be limited if you only approached the changes agreed to as a project plan. You would miss the sustaining power of a networked team committed to your vision—continually learning, sharing, creating and collaborating. The focus on women is then infused into all fundraising processes and practices and updated when more is learned.

> We found that momentum for change and long-term sustainability increased the more we abandoned delivery ideas of action planning, monitoring progress, and building implementation strategies. Our experience suggests that organizational change needs to look a lot more like an inspired movement than a neatly packaged or engineered product. (Cooperrider and Whitney 2005, 34)

This commitment of the whole system (leaders, staff, key stakeholders, etc.) to the compelling vision is what will accelerate women's philanthropy for your organization. The commitment of the whole system is also what will sustain the changes ahead. You are now in the thick of behavior and process change. We know change is not easy. People will forget. Something will be overlooked. There will be missteps. There will be complaints. But there will be steps forward, too, successes that happen more quickly than expected and stronger relationships at all levels. The commitment of the whole keeps each person, team and the entire organization oriented toward trying again and again, until the chosen mindsets and actions become the new normal.

The College of William & Mary chose the Appreciative Inquiry approach to open up everyone's engagement to increase women's philanthropy. After the discovery and dream were created, 100 staff members were trained in

Appreciative Inquiry and asked to design their own team's part in meeting the overarching vision. A month after the training, a meeting was convened to focus on an alumni couple. The gift officer presented recommended strategies, but only for the husband. That blind spot was pointed out by other departments in the meeting; the village focused on women had already grown organically.

Destiny Approach

Throughout this chapter, I will use the William & Mary Appreciative Inquiry training workshop as an example to showcase how to create your destiny. Matthew Lambert, vice president of advancement at William & Mary, wanted to inspire change rapidly across the culture. He shared with me:

> I believe that our focus on women and philanthropy is central to a strategy of building a culture of engagement and philanthropy. I wanted a thoughtful, strategic approach to women's philanthropy. And I wanted change with momentum, but that would last. Therefore, I knew we needed a multi-dimensional effort that included communication, alumni affairs, development, volunteers—the whole system. Each team needed to own its own model of how to achieve our goals. With everyone involved, we'd gain strategic alignment.

There are five key principles for destiny. These are not linear; often they are all happening at once. (For more about these principles, see: *The Power of Appreciative Inquiry: A Practical Guide to Positive Change* [2010] by Diana Whitney and Amanda Trosten-Bloom.)

Celebrate

Celebration happens throughout the process. William & Mary started the workshop by celebrating all the new information they had discovered, the powerful taskforce volunteers and staff leaders who were already engaged in the effort and the shared commitment to an overarching dream. Celebration continues whenever there is success or important changes. The example above about the team intervening in the major-donor strategy was shared, as well as the unexpectedly quick success of achieving over 100 members for the Society of 1918 in two months rather than one year. Celebrating the big and the small changes is a way to communicate that you are making progress.

Generate Ideas for Action

Actions must be tangible, yet still a stretch. Staff who think of new ideas know they are not yet happening but believe they could happen with intention and attention. These types of ideas often open up excitement and energy. During the training, each William & Mary team took on its own mini-dream and design, coming up with a list of actions. There was a buzz of energy as team members talked and wrote on flipcharts during this part of the workshop, and pride as they presented their ideas to peers on the other teams.

Self-Organize for Action

Appreciative inquiry is not a top-down model. Those on the front-lines have to self-organize around change. William & Mary trained everyone in advancement with this principle in mind. Lambert did not tell them what to do. Instead, each team (communications, alumni affairs, annual fund, major gift officers, prospect management, etc.) developed its own actionable, achievable vision that served advancement's overarching goals. When the teams presented to the full group, they found opportunities to assist each other, such as alumni affairs realizing it needed a consistent process to share stories about women it met with the communications team. Each team took its chosen actions seriously and created next steps after the training.

Establish a Supporting Infrastructure

I've shared that hiring a staff member to run a "women's philanthropy program" does not work in isolation. One person cannot make the organizational changes needed for sustainability, and that is why many early programs floundered. However, when someone is hired to lead the initiative and provide support to the many team projects, then you have someone leading a whole system change. William & Mary hired Valerie Cushman to be the director of alumnae initiatives. Cushman works with her peers by coaching, nudging, documenting, communicating updates, integrating activities, helping with strategies, celebrating achievements and helping to open doors to women prospects as needed.

Here is a note Cushman sent out right after the Appreciative Inquiry training:

> I will follow-up with each of the AVPs [team leads] over the next two weeks with the following goals:

1. To discuss the conversations and outcomes of the work of your own team (your direct reports);
2. To talk about how I can assist as you complete the next steps by April 29 and in preparation for our May leadership meeting;
3. To review the summary spreadsheet for areas where your team has been noted as a stakeholder;
4. To talk about how we can best track and share "drops that are already in the bucket" so we can promote work well done.

Cushman has the backing of all the associate vice presidents in advancement, the executive director of the alumni association, the vice present of advancement and, through him, support of the president, provost, deans and board of visitors. Cushman is integrated, as needed, into conversations and decisions on women's philanthropy at all levels.

Learning and Expanding

William & Mary's focus on women's engagement and philanthropy has spread beyond just advancement. In the individual colleges, they are looking at the number of women nominated for advisory boards, awards given to alumnae, leadership development for volunteers, etc. This expansion requires continual attention to discover the facts about the current processes and then redesign behaviors, systems and structures to be adapted to align with the overarching vision.

Destiny Example

What does this work look like at the macro and micro level?

William & Mary's advancement leadership team took into account what they learned during discovery and created a compelling vision for all:

William & Mary honors the power of women. They are involved in every facet of the university's success. Recognizing their central role in engagement and philanthropy, women will represent 50 percent of volunteer leaders and private giving by 2020. By increasing their active participation in all aspects of university life, William & Mary will create a culture that empowers women and enhances their impact on campus and community. The Alma Mater of the Nation will serve as a global model for others who strive to produce and celebrate women leaders.

This macro vision was shared in the Appreciative Inquiry training. Across the full day, six teams discussed the discovery information, the overarching vision, and went to work on their roles to support the vision.

Here is the plan of one of those six teams—the Prospect Development and Information Strategy Office.

The team vision they created at the training became their project summary:

The PD&IS team is committed to helping W&M Advancement achieve its vision of reaching a 50 percent representation of women as volunteer leaders and private donors by 2020, with W&M serving as a global model for others who strive to produce and celebrate women leaders. The following action plan details our initiatives for new policies and procedures that encourage equitable focus on our alumnae and alumni spouses with regard to engagement, board service, volunteerism and giving. Our goal is to provide dedicated research and portfolio management to help gift officers have more diverse portfolios and a more inclusive picture of women as philanthropists and couples as joint donors, regardless of the spouse's education or employment status.

They designed a more specific objective:

To establish new policies and procedures for research and prospect management, specifically addressing how we identify, assign, track and report on the female and minority alums as volunteers, leaders and donors, directly helping our Advancement team to reach our vision of 50 percent representation by 2020.

Note that they added minorities to their work, understanding that certain changes they'd implement for women could also be applied to serve other segments of prospects and households, like the LGBT community and minorities. Under each design choice they had made, the PD&IS team then wrote specific actions to take. I'm highlighting only a few of the many actions they committed to:

- Prospect Management:
  - Review of gift officer portfolios and prospect pools to ensure an equal representation of women and minorities.
  - Add percentage of men vs. women to the PD&IS Quarterly Review Executive Summary Reports.

- General Research:
  - Increase focus on uncovering relevant information on women.
  - Redesign how we pull lists of prospects.

- Profile Reports and Briefings:
  - Edit reports and briefings to focus equally on both members in a household.
  - Edit reports to include all philanthropy in the household, not just one person's.

- Wealth Inventory:
  - Include any special interests held by a spouse, as it may guide household's decision-making.
  - Research previous names of all household members, as records may not have been updated or assets may be under a separate professional identity.
  - Include current and past employment of both spouses/partners.

The team created a Microsoft project plan to establish deadlines and track progress. They designated a project lead as well as a project team to support the work.

Note that Cushman did not need to lead any PD&IS work. The PD&IS team was fully in charge of executing its own plan. In fact, ONLY that team could execute this plan. Cushman is not an expert in research or data pulls or how best to balance and track portfolios. The members of the PD&IS team were hired for this specific expertise. They are the individuals doing critical work that will impact fundraising portfolios, research and the quality of information about donors and prospects. All of this will impact systemic blind spots and increase the visibility of and knowledge about women who may care to support William & Mary with all their resources.

This is Appreciative Inquiry at its best: creating an alignment across all the strengths *already in place* within the organization to help achieve a transformative vision. This strategic framework and approach frees up personal *and* organizational potential. The strengths, commitment and expertise of the PD&IS team were freed up to contribute to William & Mary's overarching vision.

I'm obviously a believer in the power of Appreciative Inquiry to create lasting change. Moreover, I also believe that Appreciative Inquiry is particularly suited to help accelerate women's philanthropy. This book has outlined that many women prefer to learn, be a partner, contribute with all their resources, work organically with others and focus on change rather than titles or hierarchy. When women come together to make change, there is a surge of energy, connection, creativity and new ideas. Powerful and sustained change can happen from women.

Appreciative inquiry can bring forward the same results for your organization. It, too, produces a surge of energy, connection, creativity and new ideas. People at all levels of the organization come together with their expertise and commitment into new collaborations, learning and partnership. Powerful and sustained changes never thought possible by one person are suddenly taking place across the organization.

What About . . . ?

As you move along the path of your women's philanthropy vision, challenges and questions will naturally come up. At a meeting of seven directors of women's philanthropy initiatives gathered with Andrea Pactor, associate director of the Women's Philanthropy Institute, the group discussed issues they were grappling with:

- How do we build more internal champions for the initiative across the organization, not just in our development departments?
- How can we work with women donors as full partners when their ideas may be ahead of the organization?
- How do we engage our growing pool of women philanthropists who now want to do more to help?
- How do we tackle diversity? Women's philanthropy is not only about white, upper-middle-class women.
- How might we encourage multigenerational giving? The younger women in the family approach giving differently than their mothers.

When you are overwhelmed by success (many new women donors who now want further engagement) or challenges, turn to the Appreciative Inquiry model. Each of these questions is an ideal topic for an Appreciative Inquiry exercise. An Appreciative Inquiry mindset will help you find the road forward, sometimes in just a few hours, with the right people around the table. What do you need to discover about the issue? Who else needs to be involved? What is your compelling dream for the issue; what could happen beyond your current imagination? What design elements will help you get there? And what steps and stakeholders will create your destiny? You'll find that the Appreciative Inquiry model can work with broad systems change as well as specific issues such as deeper engagement from a campaign steering committee. When you ask for people's participation and stories and when they are part of creating their own compelling vision and designs, you've opened up a team's good will and desire to contribute.

Melissa Effron Hayek, director of women and philanthropy at the University of California, Los Angeles, instinctively used the power of this framework to reboot their program at UCLA. While she didn't call it Appreciative Inquiry, she used the same core approach. The year 2014 was the 20th anniversary of UCLA's women's philanthropy program. It had become a women's membership program where women were asked to become members. Many questions had come up over time. Since members were asked to join when they gave $25,000 or more, why should they join? What was the benefit to them? What was the benefit to the university? Why was it valuable to be part of this group? They found that many women donors were declining the invitation. The staff and board members agreed it was time for a review.

They started with an internal assessment by the staff and senior leadership of the membership and a review of current programs. They also took time to review the latest research on women's giving and best practices of other programs. The board president had been a high-level executive and skilled facilitator who brought the discovery information to the newly convened membership review committee of past board presidents. Armed with this background, they envisioned a transformational shift. The program would become inclusive and more expansive.

This vision led to the following design elements:

- Women were automatically included as members if they made a gift of $25,000 or a five-year pledge of $5,000 per year for a five-year membership. This made the membership more accessible. These members will be approached at the end of their term to reinvest in the university and retain their membership. This is used as a tool to encourage more women to give at this level to join the group. Membership grew from 145 to 2,300 women.

- A new lifetime member level was created to recognize women whose giving reached $250,000. Their membership is in perpetuity.

- High-level female campus leaders were made honorary members (making it easier for members to hear about their work and for them to develop relationships with major donors).

- Two honorary spots on the board were created for young alumnae to increase their exposure to this philanthropic group and give valuable input.
- University staff created more consistent and personal programming. They heard during the discovery phase and from a subsequent survey that members were not interested in social media or email "touches," but instead wanted to connect with each other and learn about the university and different interesting topics.

The process of developing this model and shifting took six months, but it broadened the depth and breadth of the number of women connected with the initiative. The members felt they were listened to and trusted the process as it unfolded, which increased their buy-in to the changes. Their input also brought about far superior ideas and strategies. This approach significantly increased the scope of those supporting it across UCLA. Throughout this redesign, Hayek, the director of women and philanthropy, had leadership support all the way up to the university chancellor's wife, who even became a member of the board. She also had support across the organization. Hayek's peers saw how this network could benefit their departments (annual giving, major giving, regional outreach) and increased their connections to and partnerships with Hayek and the program. This broader collaboration was being put in place when UCLA began its 100th anniversary campaign in 2014. The focus of the campaign has been funding *and* participation, and the women and philanthropy program has played a key role for both goals. The program has also provided leadership and diversity on various campaign committees.

Results for You

At this point, you may be asking, "So, what results will I see?" You *will* see results, but I am purposely not going to provide examples of how many dollars have been raised from women by the many organizations I cite throughout this book. Certainly, it is in the hundreds of millions collectively. However, to cite only the financial resources gained by this transformative, participatory approach would be a disservice to the very intent of this book, and the strong desire that women hold that they be seen for *all* the resources they might offer.

Instead, let me share that as you achieve your destiny, you will gain multiple results. These results include, but aren't limited to:

- Increased funding from women
- Increased funding from men (remember, when you reach women, you reach men too)
- Deeper relationships with donors
- Expertise from volunteers
- Engaged partners who bring forward new potential partners
- Increased pipeline of women prospects
- Creative new engagement programs
- Women leaders for your councils and boards
- External visibility for your mission
- Diversity
- Networks
- Cross-team collaborations
- Metrics and evaluation of results
- Ongoing inquiry, imagination and innovation

I can promise you that you will "solve" your desire to increase women's philanthropy for your cause and gain so much more. You will grow more capacity, on so many levels, to accelerate *your mission's vision*. And that is what growing your engagement with and support from women is really all about.

Results for Our Society

The goal of this book is to translate what we know about how women give into new fundraising behaviors and outcomes. It starts with each one of us being intentional in our roles, on our teams, across our organizations.

Imagine if the changes at your organization were combined with similar changes at every university, school and nonprofit across this country. Imagine if every organization adapted their fundraising. What would be possible in this country if engagement of women became the norm everywhere?

First, we would no longer be talking about "women's philanthropy." We wouldn't have to cite statistics and create a compelling case to focus on women. Women would be represented equally at the table at our universities and nonprofits. We wouldn't have to push for diversity. How we connect with women would be so essential to fundraising that it would be embodied in us and our normal habits. Our processes and conversations with women would not take extra effort, because we'd be choosing what resonates without pause, consistently and with great success.

Second, we would be raising significantly more funding across the non-profit sector. Andrea Pactor of the Women's Philanthropy Institute shared with me recently that we could grow individual giving in this country by 5 percent if women contributed 1 percent of the $14 trillion in current assets they hold for charitable purposes. (This would quickly add $14 billion to the annual number tracked by Giving USA.) With this infusion of funding, so much more is possible to address the social issues in our communities and across our country.

Third, we would have *all* the resources from the other half of the population welcomed at the table. The growth, and frankly repairs, needed in our civic society require far more than money. We must add new voices, discernment, leadership, innovation, commitment, collaborations and partnerships to solve pressing issues and divisions in our country. Although rarely documented, women across history have been a significant force for social change. Reforms such as abolition, temperance and suffrage occurred during historical periods when women were still marginalized. Imagine the acceleration of solutions that might unfold when the full support of women and men is evenly balanced across our philanthropic sector. As shared in the introduction, Agnus Gund held this vision and acted on it, in partnership with many women and men, to address high rates of incarceration and recidivism in the United States. Many other issues will be transformed with this same breadth of support.

We fundraise to improve the greater good for all in our world. Yet we've approached the societal issues with one hand tied behind our backs, using unconsciously dated and biased approaches that may not resonate with half our population. It is time to untie our hands and stretch together to discover, dream and design new fundraising approaches for women, opening the way for them to take their rightful place in philanthropic efforts to better our world. The destiny of our civil society is at stake.

REFERENCES

Preface

Switzer, Cody. 2017. "6 Things Charities Should Know About America's Rapid Demographic Shift." *The Chronicle of Philanthropy*, June 8.

Introduction

Cooperrider, David and Diana Whitney. 2005. *Appreciative Inquiry: A Positive Revolution in Change*. Oakland: Berrett-Koehler Publishers.

Donnelly, Shannon. 2018. "Vecellios' Gift Will Establish Women's Cardiology Research Fund." *Palm Beach Daily News*, February 5.

Libbey, Peter. 2017. "Art for Justice Fund Awards $22 Million in Grants." *The New York Times*, November 15.

Chapter 1

Brown, Brené. 2015. *Rising Strong*. New York: Random House.

Bureau of Labor Statistics. 2011. *Spotlight: Women at Work*. BLS.gov. Last modified March 2011. https://www.bls.gov/spotlight/2011/women.

Bureau of Labor Statistics. 2014. *Women in the Labor Force: A Databook*. BLS.gov. Last modified December 9, 2016. https://www.bls.gov/opub/reports/womens-databook /archive/women-in-the-labor-force-a-databook-2014.pdf.

Center on Philanthropy at Indiana University. 2011. *2011 Study of High Net Worth Women's Philanthropy and the Impact of Women's Giving Networks*. Center on Philanthropy at Indiana University. Last modified December 2011. http://hdl .handle.net/1805/5682.

Cooperrider and Whitney 2005.

Gill, Preeti. 2018. "Donations at the Diva Level." *Diversity Driven Data*. Last modified April 5, 2018. https://diversitydrivendata.blog/donations-at-the-diva-level.

IRS. 2007. *SOI Tax Stats—Female Top Wealthholders by Size of Net Worth*. IRS.gov. Last modified February 7, 2018. https://www.irs.gov/statistics/soi-tax-stats-female-top-wealthholders-by-size-of-net-worth.

Kayembe, Danielle. 2017. "The Silent Rise of the Female-Driven Economy." *Refinery29*, Last modified December 20, 2017. https://www.refinery29.com/2017/12/184334/rise-of-female-driven-economy-feminist-economics?bucketed=true.

Lenok, David H. 2016. *Increasingly, Women Control Wealth and Charities Benefit*. WealthManagement.com. Last modified March 11, 2016. http://www.wealthmanagement.com/high-net-worth/increasingly-women-control-wealth-and-charities-benefit.

Lofquist, Daphne, Terry Lugaila, Martin O'Connell, and Sarah Feliz. 2012. *Households and Families: 2010*. U.S. Census Bureau. Last modified April 2012. https://www.census.gov/prod/cen2010/briefs/c2010br-14.pdf.

Mesch, Debra. 2010a. *Women Give 2010: New Research about Women and Giving*. The Women's Philanthropy Institute. Last modified October 2010. http://hdl.handle.net/1805/6337.

———. 2010b. *Women Give 2010 Part 2: Causes Women Support*. The Women's Philanthropy Institute. Last modified December 2012. http://hdl.handle.net/1805/6338.

———. 2016. "The Gender Gap in Charitable Giving." *The Wall Street Journal*, February 1.

Mesch, Debra, Una Osili, Jacqueline Ackerman, and Elizabeth Dale. 2015a. *How and Why Women Give: Current and Future Directions for Research on Women's Philanthropy*. The Women's Philanthropy Institute. Last modified May 2015. http://hdl.handle.net/1805/6983.

———. 2015b. *Where Do Men and Women Give? Gender Differences in the Motivations and Purposes for Charitable Giving*. The Women's Philanthropy Institute. Last modified September 2015. http://hdl.handle.net/1805/6985.

Mesch, Debra, Mark Ottoni-Wilhelm, Una Osili, Xiao Han, Andrea Pactor, Jacqueline Ackerman, Jacqueline and Kathryn Tolley. 2016. *Women Give 2016*. The Women's Philanthropy Institute. Last modified November 15, 2016. http://hdl.handle.net/1805/11446.

O'Connor, Heather, Debra Mesch, Una Osili, Andrea Pactor, Jacqueline Ackerman, Elizabeth Dale, and Diana Small. 2018. *Giving by and for Women: Understanding High-Net-Worth Donors' Support for Women and Girls*. The Women's Philanthropy Institute. Last modified January 30, 2018. http://hdl.handle.net/1805/15117.

Osili, Una, Debra Mesch, Linh Preston, Cagla Okten, Jonathan Bergdoll, Jacqueline Ackerman, and Andrea Pactor. 2017. *Gender Differences in #GivingTuesday Participation*. The Women's Philanthropy Institute. Last modified December 12, 2017. http://hdl.handle.net/1805/14782.

Strang, Lynne. 2011. "Hate Networking? Try 'NetWeaving.'" *Late Blooming Entrepreneurs*. Last modified October 10, 2011. https://latebloomingentrepreneurs.wordpress.com/2011/10/10/hate-networking-try-"netweaving".

Swank, Katherine. 2010. "'Fem-anthropy': Women's Philanthropic Giving Patterns and Objectives." *Advancing Philanthropy,* March/April.

Vespa, Jonathan. 2017. *The Changing Economics and Demographics of Young Adulthood: 1975–2016.* Census.gov. Last modified April 2017. https://www.census.gov/content /dam/Census/library/publications/2017/demo/p20-579.pdf.

Wang, Wendy, Kim Parker, and Paul Taylor. 2013. *Breadwinner Moms.* Pew Research Center. Last modified May 29, 2013. http://www.pewsocialtrends.org/2013/05/29 /breadwinner-moms.

Wells Fargo (Wells Fargo Investment Institute). 2017. *Women and Investing: Building on Strengths.* Wells Fargo Media. Last modified July 2017. https://www08 .wellsfargomedia.com/assets/pdf/personal/investing/investment-institute/women -and-investing-ADA.pdf.

Witter, Lisa and Lisa Chen. 2008. *The She Spot: Why Women are the Market for Changing the World—And How to Reach Them.* San Francisco: Berrett-Koehler Publishers.

Chapter 2

Carter, Nancy M. and Harvey M. Wagner. 2011. *The Bottom Line: Corporate Performance and Women's Representation on Boards (2004–2008).* Catalyst. Last modified March 1, 2011. http://www.catalyst.org/knowledge/bottom-line-corporate -performance-and-womens-representation-boards-20042008.

Cook, Chris. 2013. *What's the Problem? (No. Strike That.) What's Working Here?* Capiche.us. Last modified January 31, 2013. http://capiche.us/2013 /what%E2%80%99s-the-problem-no-strike-that-what%E2%80%99s-working-here.

Chapter 3

Di Mento, Maria. 2014. "Lack of Women in Top Roles Hinders Nonprofits, Female Nonprofit Workers Say." *Chronicle of Philanthropy,* April 28. https://www .philanthropy.com/article/Lack-of-Women-in-Top-Roles/153197.

Lambert, Matthew. 2016. *Engaging Women in Philanthropy: Practical Ways to Shift Our Approach.* Academic Impressions. Last modified June 15, 2016. https://www .academicimpressions.com/engaging-women-in-philanthropy-practical-ways-to -shift-our-approach.

Tempel, Eugene R., Timothy L. Seiler, and Dwight F. Burlingame. 2016. *Achieving Excellence in Fundraising.* Hoboken: Wiley.

Chapter 4

Mesch, Debra and Andrea Pactor. 2009. *Women's Philanthropy on Campus.* The Women's Philanthropy Institute. Last modified December 2009. http://hdl.handle .net/1805/6261.

Chapter 5

Strozzi Institute. *Declarations—Designing a Future.* StrozziInstitute.com. Last modified June 2016. https://strozziinstitute.com/wp-content/uploads/2016/06/Declarations -DesigningaFuture2016.pdf.

Chapter 8

Gill, Preeti. 2015. *What About Women?* Prospect Research Institute.

Mesch, Debra and Una Osili 2013. *Women Give 2013: New Research on Charitable Giving by Girls and Boys.* The Women's Philanthropy Institute. Last modified 2013. http://hdl.handle.net/1805/6340.

Chapter 9

Bekkers, René and Pamala Wiepking. 2011. "A Literature Review of Empirical Studies of Philanthropy." *Nonprofit and Voluntary Sector Quarterly* 40 (5): 924–973. https://doi.org/10.1177/0899764010380927.

Gilmore, James and Joseph B. Pine. 2007. *Authenticity: What Consumers Really Want.* Boston: Harvard Business School Press.

Goldman, Bruce. 2017. "Two Minds: The Cognitive Differences Between Men and Women." *Stanford Medicine,* Spring. https://stanmed.stanford.edu/2017spring/how -mens-and-womens-brains-are-different.html.

Hodge, James. 2012. *Philanthropy & Relationships.* Indianapolis: The Center on Philanthropy at Indiana University.

Mesch, et al. 2015a.

Tannen, Deborah. 2010. "He Said, She Said." *Scientific American Mind,* May/June. https://www.scientificamerican.com/article/he-said-she-said.

Chapter 10

Center on Philanthropy. 2011. 2011 Study of High Net Worth: Women's Philanthropy and the Impact of Women's Giving Networks. http://hdl.handle.net/1805/5682.

Gaia, Prema. 2017. "'Tend and Befriend': How Hope for the World Is Growing in Circles." *Spirituality & Health,* October 18. https://spiritualityhealth.com/articles /2017/10/18/tend-befriend.

Mesch, et al. 2015a.

Mesch and Osili. 2013.

O'Connor, et al. 2018.

Shaw-Hardy, Sondra, Martha A. Taylor, and Buffy Beaudoin-Schwartz. 2010. *Women & Philanthropy: Boldly Shaping a Better World.* Hoboken: Wiley.

Chapter 11

Bearman, Jessica, Julia Carboni, Angela Eikenberry, and Jason Franklin. 2017. *The Landscape of Giving Circles/Collective Giving Groups in the U.S.* Collective Giving Research Group. Last modified November 14, 2017. http://hdl.handle.net/1805/14527.

Center on Philanthropy. 2011.

Collier, Charles. 2012. *Wealth in Families.* Cambridge: President and Fellows of Harvard College.

Damisch, Peter, Monish Kumar, Anna Zakrzewski, and Natalia Zhiglinskaya. 2010. *Leveling the Playing Field: Upgrading the Wealth Management Experience for Women.* The Boston Consulting Group (July).

Economist Intelligence Unit. 2018. "Sisterhood Is Powerful—and Now It's Also Wealthy." *The Economist,* January 9. http://sustainablegiving.economist.com /sisterhood-is-powerful-and-now-its-also-wealthy.

Eikenberry, Angela M. and Jessica Bearman. 2009. *The Impact of Giving Together: Giving Circles' Influence on Members' Philanthropic and Civic Behaviors, Knowledge and Attitudes.* Forum of Regional Association of Grantmakers. Last modified May 2009. http://hdl.handle.net/1805/5664.

Houssian, Jessica. 2016. "Tapping the Great Potential of Female Philanthropists." *Stanford Social Innovation Review,* March 17. https://ssir.org/articles/entry/tapping _the_great_potential_of_female_philanthropists.

Mesch, Debra, Una Osili, Andrea Pactor, Jacqueline Ackerman, Jonathan Bergdoll, and Elizabeth Dale. 2016. *Giving to Women and Girls: Who Gives, and Why?* The Women's Philanthropy Institute. Last modified May 24, 2016. http://hdl.handle.net /1805/9624.

O'Connor, et al. 2018.

Rockefeller Philanthropy Advisors. 2017. *Women and Giving.* Rockefeller Philanthropy Advisors. Last modified August 2017. http://www.rockpa.org/wp-content/uploads /2017/08/Women-and-Giving.pdf.

Schiller, Ronald J. 2013. *The Chief Development Officer: Beyond Fundraising.* Plymouth: Rowman & Littlefield Education.

———. 2016. *Belief and Confidence: Donors Talk about Successful Philanthropic Partnership.* Washington, D.C.: Council for Advancement and Support of Education.

U.S. Trust. 2013. *Insights on Wealth and Worth™: Women and Wealth Fact Sheet.* Accessed April 10, 2018. http://www.ncgs.org/Pdfs/Resources/Women%20and%20 Wealth.pdf.

———. 2014. *2014 U.S. Trust Insights on Wealth and Worth™: Women and Wealth.*

———. 2016. U.S. *Trust Study of High Net Worth Philanthropy.* Accessed April 10, 2018. http://newsroom.bankofamerica.com/files/press_kit/additional/2016_US_Trust _Study_of_High_Net_Worth_Philanthropy_-_Executive_Summary.pdf.

Wells Fargo. 2017.

Chapter 12

Cooperrider and Whitney. 2005.

Hawthorne, Fran. 2012. "In Pursuit of the Female Philanthropists," *The New York Times*, November 8.

O'Connor, et al. 2018.

Whitney, Diana and Amanda Trosten-Bloom. 2010. *The Power of Appreciative Inquiry: A Practical Guide to Positive Change*. Oakland: Berrett-Koehler Publishers.

Witter and Chen. 2008.

INDEX

C

DEDICATION AND ACKNOWLEDGMENTS

Dedication

I dedicate this book to the Women's Philanthropy Institute, its past leadership and in particular its current leaders: Dr. Debra Mesch, director, and Andrea Pactor, associate director. You have advanced women's philanthropy through original, rigorous research that informs donors, fundraisers and institutions. Thanks to an incredible body of empirical research that has grown significantly in the past decade, the world now knows that *gender matters* in philanthropy. This book would not have been possible without the solid ground you laid.

Acknowledgments

The Merriam-Webster dictionary defines *philanthropy* as "goodwill to (other) members of the human race; especially: active effort to promote human welfare." I am grateful to every woman who is a philanthropist per this definition. Thank you for bringing all your resources, of which money is one part, to make this world a better place. Thank you for your activism, voice, donations and focus on preserving the dignity and welfare in our communities and across our country and world. You are needed more than ever.

I also express my gratitude to the numerous women (and men) who have inspired me across my career. I heard your stories at Cornell University, the American Red Cross and in many focus groups and interviews. Your experiences, frustrations, guidance and ideas have filled my mind and inspired my writing. Thank you for your time and honesty. This book is built around what you desire in your philanthropic partnerships with causes you care about.

Philanthropy starts at home. When parents are role models for the children to witness the power and joy produced when helping others, there is a much higher likelihood that children will also give back when they are adults. Thank you, Mom and Dad, for exposing me and my siblings to opportunities to be of service to others and for being my role models. Your values were present at every dinner—family, education, faith, making a difference. I followed your footsteps, Mom, to become a fundraiser and creator. I'm grateful you showed me the way.

Treasured colleagues have helped shaped this book. The following people were a consistent "Yes!" in providing time, advice and insights: Andrea Pactor at WPI, Valerie Cushman and Sue Warner at the College of William & Mary, Beth Mann at the Jewish Federations of North America, Bridget Booher at Duke University, Leslie Wetzel at the University of San Francisco, Melissa Effron Hayek at the University of California, Los Angeles and Mindi Laine at Dartmouth College. Numerous others were interviewed as well. I so appreciate what you shared as you enriched my thinking and added depth to this book. Finally, I am grateful to Martha Taylor at the University of Wisconsin Foundation and co-founder of WPI for mentoring me in women's philanthropy. I am humbled to build on her great work, as well as that of Sondra Shaw-Hardy, also co-founder of WPI, and many others.

Many thanks also to Orr Associates, Inc. Across the span of two years, you supported me and a nimble team to partner with five universities and nonprofits and help them design the strategy for each of their women's philanthropy efforts. This was a time-compressed, rich period that quickly revealed what worked, or not, as we helped each client.

More than the influence of my professional work and colleagues is infused in this book. I would not have a systems lens were it not for important training I received throughout my life. The Hoffman Institute taught me that an individual is more than one's intellect—the combined system of the spirit, body, emotions and intellect is needed in equal parts for growth and transformation. I was trained in Appreciative Inquiry by Ralph Weickel and the Corporation for Positive Change. This whole-systems approach builds on the unique strengths and values of each organization, plus the engagement of many parts of the system, to make sustained change. Most profoundly, I was trained and transformed by the Strozzi institute. What I learned about aligning purpose with conscious action lives in me in every conversation. I gained the competency to discern what may have shaped individuals and teams, face directly into reality and help bring forward new practices and capacities to align with and achieve new visions. I am eternally grateful to Richard Strozzi-Heckler, Staci Haines and my many teachers and coaches at the Strozzi Institute.

My ability to write about women as change agents—for that is what women philanthropists are—comes from my decades with amazing women who have been influencers and anchors in my life. I have benefitted from a valued web of Francesca Balada (my daughter), Anne Loehr and Mary Loehr (my sisters), and Susan Dunlap, Dana Pulley, Bebe Hansen, Paula Peter, Vally Kovary, Shelley Semmler, Kathie Hunt, Jen Alpert, Tara DeNuccio and Debra Niewald—all good friends. We have traveled through the fires and joys of life together, and each been transformed. I am proof that the commitment of any one woman can be amplified when she is held and supported by her personal tribe of strong women.

This book was molded by generous readers and editors. Thank you, Carrie Koplinka-Loehr and Mary Kate Robbett for your discerning questions, insightful comments and bold editing each step of the way. Linda Cashdan was a consistent support for edits throughout the draft phases, and Darcia Bowman from CASE made strategic copy edits to help the final book shine. I also appreciated cheerleading from my wonderful blended family—many thanks to Kaitlyn Coray Bell, Jakob Coray and all the Corays and Loehrs.

Finally, this book, my first, would not have happened without Kevin Coray, my husband. You are proof that a strong man can fully support a strong woman. You are my biggest advocate, a patient and committed listener, an editor of this manuscript, a consistent source of ideas and breakthroughs who added depth to my use of Appreciative Inquiry, thanks to your own training in this work. And you were a true partner in keeping the rest of our life running smoothly while I wrote. Thank you, my love.

And now, dear reader, take all that I offer in this book and run with it. As Mahatma Gandhi said, "You must be the change you wish to see in the world." Don't miss this moment. Women are done waiting on the sidelines.

ABOUT THE AUTHOR

Kathleen Loehr is the principal of Kathleen Loehr & Associates, a philanthropy and leadership practice based in Alexandria, Virginia. Her partnership with nonprofit leaders and philanthropists is grounded by 35 years in the nonprofit sector. She understands the benefits and joys of nonprofit work, as well as the complexities and challenges of changes in the sector.

Kathleen is chair of the Advisory Council for the Women's Philanthropy Institute at the Lilly Family School of Philanthropy at Indiana University. Her women's philanthropy expertise results from her strategic partnership to engage more women at universities (Cornell University, University of San Francisco, Duke University, The College of William & Mary), nonprofits (Women Moving Millions, the Jewish Federation of Greater Philadelphia, the National Women's History Museum), sororities (Alpha Chi Omega Foundation, the Alpha Phi Foundation) and girls' schools (Louise S. McGehee School). She is also a regular speaker for CASE conferences on women's philanthropy.

Kathleen was a C-suite leader of fundraising for the American Red Cross, Save the Children, the International Crisis Group, and key departments at Cornell University. Consulting partners have included national nonprofits such as the Girl Scouts, The Salvation Army and the Jewish Federations of North America as well as community nonprofits serving children, youth, vulnerable families and the homeless.

As a master somatic coach, certified through the Strozzi Institute, Kathleen is pragmatic and relational. Nonprofits value that she understands their goals and brings empathy, honesty, practical experience and powerful questions to help them make choices that support their visions. She also is a trusted advisor to nonprofit leaders and family foundations. Through individual and facilitated group work, she helps blend their aspirations to serve the common good with the commitment to create effective and sustained impact. Trained in Appreciative Inquiry, Kathleen combines nonprofit and fundraising expertise, coaching and strategy to help individuals and groups navigate change.

Kathleen holds a bachelor's degree in Government from Cornell University's College of Arts and Sciences. She is a board member for the Center for Disaster Philanthropy.

More than work has shaped Kathleen. Growing up in a family of 10, she learned to effectively build relationships up, down and out. Her humanitarian focus came from living abroad in Bolivia and Italy, as well as extensive travels in Africa, Europe and Central/South America, where she has witnessed human dignity in the face of extreme poverty. Finally, the curiosity in her is kept alive by paying attention to the questions and passions of the millenials, Generation Z and children in her big, blended family.

For more information: www.kathleenloehr.com/

ABOUT CASE

The **Council for Advancement and Support of Education (CASE)** is the professional organization for advancement professionals at all levels who work in alumni relations, communications and marketing, development and advancement services.

CASE's membership includes nearly 3,700 colleges, universities, and independent elementary and secondary schools in more than 80 countries. This makes CASE one of the largest nonprofit education associations in the world in terms of institutional membership. CASE serves more than 88,000 advancement professionals on the staffs of member institutions.

CASE has offices in Washington, D.C., London, Singapore and Mexico City. The association produces high-quality and timely content, publications, conferences, institutes and workshops that assist advancement professionals in performing more effectively and serving their institutions.